Dipak Barman
Subashish Bhattacharjee

Contemporary Women's Fiction

Feminist Narratives in Selected
Twentieth Century Women's Novels

Anchor Academic
Publishing

Barman, Dipak, Bhattacharjee, Subashish: Contemporary Women's Fiction. Feminist Narratives in Selected Twentieth Century Women's Novels, Hamburg, Anchor Academic Publishing 2016

Buch-ISBN: 978-3-96067-027-8
PDF-eBook-ISBN: 978-3-96067-527-3
Druck/Herstellung: Anchor Academic Publishing, Hamburg, 2016

Bibliografische Information der Deutschen Nationalbibliothek:
Die Deutsche Nationalbibliothek verzeichnet diese Publikation in der Deutschen Nationalbibliografie; detaillierte bibliografische Daten sind im Internet über http://dnb.d-nb.de abrufbar.

Bibliographical Information of the German National Library:
The German National Library lists this publication in the German National Bibliography. Detailed bibliographic data can be found at: http://dnb.d-nb.de

© Anchor Academic Publishing, Imprint der Diplomica Verlag GmbH
Hermannstal 119k, 22119 Hamburg
http://www.diplomica-verlag.de, Hamburg 2016
Printed in Germany

About the Book

Women's writing in the twentieth century has shown a dramatic shift in its preoccupations and intentions. Rather than occupying itself with the trivialities of the social and domestic spheres, the writing by women in the latter half of the twentieth century and approaching the twenty-first century inheres concerns such as political, historical, questions of gender equity and rights, interrogations of normative and patriarchal practices and other such issues that have not been adequately addressed in women's writing thus far. The four essays in the present volume are certainly not exhaustive or adequate in this regard — that of addressing this lacuna in literary scholarship — but it may be viewed as a attempt to bridge the proverbial gap. As a precursor to further scholarly works in the area, already existing as well as forthcoming, the essays discuss the works of Toni Morrison, Margaret Atwood, Bapsi Sidhwa, Manju Kapur and Sunanda Sikdar. Although the essays purport to exploring select areas of the authors' oeuvre, the distinctive fictional structures of the authors help us to explore wider theoretical and critical issues such as postmodernity, postcolonialism, feminism, globalism, nationalism and other related issues.

About the Authors

Subashish Bhattacharjee is a UGC-Research Fellow and Teaching Assistant at the Department of English, University of North Bengal, India. He is also Visiting Faculty at Cooch Behar Panchanan Barma University and University of North Bengal, Jalpaiguri Campus. He has numerous publications to his credit including the two co-edited volumes *Postcolonial Approaches to Literature* and *Reading Literature through Feminist Lens*, both published in 2015. He is also the founder and Editor of *The Apollonian: A Journal of Interdisciplinary Studies*.

Dipak Barman is a Research Scholar at the Department of English, University of North Bengal, India. He has formerly been a Guest Faculty at ABN Seal College, University of North Bengal. He has published several articles in reputed journals and edited books, and presented papers in seminars.

CONTENTS

ACKNOWLEDGEMENTS

We would like to thank our teachers, especially at the university, who have inspired us significantly to engage with issues more critically and interrogatively. We would like to acknowledge the inspiration of Prof G.N. Ray especially—a teacher and guide who has striven to endow us with the values that he himself abides by. This book is also a small dedication to him.

We would like to thank out parents for their patience, cooperation and understanding in our efforts.

Our colleagues at respective places of employment deserve mention and acknowledgement for their support.

INTRODUCTION:
THE SPACE OF/FOR WOMEN'S WRITING

Women's fiction as a genre in itself is a rather late development, with a gamut of postcolonial and postmodern women authors producing the largesse of the literary output attributed to this development. Women's writing generally encompasses issues that are considerably more varied than those of the mainstream authors' works: issues such as women's rights and its myriad occupancies come forth in such writings that allow a commiseration of approaches both theoretical and practical. The radicalisation of writing in the twentieth century and the increase and upsurge in women's education could be cited as some of the reasons for the literary production in this genre as well as the increase in interest in women's writing. The scope of the volume coincides with this spurt in scholarship dedicated to exploring the possibilities of women's writing.

Some of the earliest and more popular instances of women's fiction in the English language are in the works of Aphra Behn, Jane Austen, the Brontës, Elizabeth Gaskell, Elizabeth Barrett Browning, Harriet Martineau, George Eliot, and thereafter widening vastly with the onset of the twentieth century to include authorship as varied as Virginia Woolf, Dorothy Richardson, Katherine Mansfield, Muriel Spark, Iris Murdoch, Doris Lessing, Jean Rhys, Margaret Drabble, A.S. Byatt, Beryl Bainbridge and a spate of later authors who practised gradually varying techniques of approach to a woman's language. The linguistic necessity was mandated only insofar as to facilitate a distinction for the genre — although it is debatable whether there were any real world implications of the linguistic divide. However, with the evolution of women's writing moving forward from the canonical, the necessity to explore the specific territories became a more pertinent imperative on part of scholars, thus attributed to the immense spurt in scholarship specifically addressing the lacuna of investigation that takes into consideration specific studies rather than locating forced points of similarity. As has been previously noted in Dr. Chakraverty's study of women's writing: "[Women's] text have occupied a central position in all literary writings representing a high standard of social and literary theories, attempting to examine not only with technique but also with tabooed subject matters in various forms such as fiction, drama, prose and short stories" (Chakraverty 1-2).

One of the most iconic books to deal with the 'context' of women's writing, or 'literature', to be more specific, is Elaine Showalter's 1977 book, *A Literature of Their Own: English*

Women Novelists from Brontë to Lessing, maps a broader readership by specifying the literary importance of women's writing. Besides the more renowned literary representatives among the women authors of each successive period, Showalter's book is notable for its sweeping survey inclusive of remarkable women authors such as Florence Nightingale, Charlotte Yonge, Dinah Mulock Craik, Margaret Oliphant, Elizabeth Lynn Linton of the Victorian and its peripheral periods; Mary Braddon, Rhoda Broughton, and Florence Marryat of the immediate post-Victorian period, and later authors such as Sarah Grand, George Egerton, Mona Caird, Elizabeth Robins, Olive Schreiner—authors whose writings reflect a particular cultural awareness that was absent from the predominantly 'patriarchal' ordination of literature of thee previous periods. The present volume does not intend to compete with Showalter's magnificent volume, and neither do we seek to compensate for the absences in that or any subsequent volumes of critical contemplation on women writers (a substantial bibliography of such works is provided at the end of the volume). The necessity to indulge in compiling a volume like the present one arises at least partially from Showalter's comments in her seminal essay, "Feminist Criticism in the Wilderness":

> "The dominant culture need not consider the muted, except to rail against 'the woman's part' in itself. Thus we need more subtle and supple accounts of influence, not just to explain women's writing but also to understand how men's writing has resisted the acknowledgement of female precursors. [...] women's fiction can be read as a double-voiced discourse, containing a 'dominant' and a 'muted' story."
>
> (Showalter 344)

It is essential to map at times creative writings and output by sections of society considered or rendered marginal. Women's writing conforms to the very rubric of representative creative practice by a marginalised group and of a style and subjectivity that deals with an isolated section of critical or practical thought. In the words of Susie Tharu and K. Lalita:

> "We believe that a feminist literary history must map the play of forces in the imaginative worlds in which women wrote, and read their literary initiatives not as an endless repetition of present day rebellions or dreams of triumph, but as different attempts to engage with the force and the conflict of the multiple cross-cutting determinations of those worlds."
>
> (Tharu and Lalita 1993: 26)

The process of creativity, of creation and of literary production has different ethics and values for women writers who allow the proliferation of their own ideals and conditions to seep through the literary fabric as opposed to more patriarchal literary excursions where the opinions of the woman are considered as removable isotopes. Not only have women challenged the role and authority of patriarchy through their 'writing back', but they have also produced some of the most definitive and radicalised examples and instances of literary history, producing a mutinous linguistic element that acts as an ideal for emancipatory circumstances, as Beauvoir states:

> "Much more interesting are the insurgent females who have challenged this unjust society; a literature of protest can engender sincere and powerful society."
>
> (Beauvoir 718)

It is notable that all five women authors considered in this volume belong to the insurgent sections, producing non-conformist and non-pacifist literature that challenges not only the social mores and patriarchal oppression but also the ideologies that have set back women's rights, education and other contingencies farther back.

From in between the pioneers of women's writing to the present practitioners of the 'genre' we have allotted chapters to a selection of authors and their works chiefly to demonstrate the range of creative output that is possible in this era of globalisation. Modern day publishing has sought to give impetus to authors irrespective of national, regional or linguistic barriers, and the objective of this volume is to endorse that very ethos in as many ways as possible. The postcolonial, postmodern domain of fiction is rife with practitioners who have shown a consistent tendency to outdo themselves with each consecutive attempt. The following chapters in the volume are dedicated to selective readings of such authors who have shown incredible flair in their writing. Each author has been seminal in her contribution to the genre of longer works of fiction, producing some of the finest and most distinctive works of fiction in the last century, and continuing further into the present century. Besides feminist issues, the authors concern themselves with issues such as race, gender, sexuality, incest, infidelity, LGBTQ rights and issues, migration, diaspora, colonialism, postcolonialism, globalisation, education, marriage, child psychology, environment and ecology, language, religion, caste, colour, nationality, regional issues, partition, politics, statehood and affiliation, besides myriad other dimensions that assert themselves through their works. The volume is a mere introductory piece towards what is definitely a far wider area of contention, and, as we hope towards a companion volume of equally wider academic scope.

The authors covered in this volume are by no means exhaustive or definitive examples of women's writing, but rather a showcase of the evolution of this sub-genre in terms of its movement from the practitioners of the preceding centuries to those women writing at the intersection of change in the twentieth and twenty-first centuries. Authors such as Margaret Atwood, Toni Morrison, Bapsi Sidhwa, Manju Kapur, Taslima Nasreen and Sunanda Sikdar, who have been explored critically in this volume with regard to select works, are literary practitioners who have showcased remarkable literary abilities in their writing, mostly a significant oeuvre. Although Taslima Nasreen's and Sunanda Sikdar's writing is not strictly in the domain of English language writing, but it was imperative to show how the proliferation of a postcolonial ethos of fiction-making is also visible on the translation sphere. The transnationalism of the two authors' translated works and their importance in postcolonial studies presently produces the ambit of theoretical conduit necessary to approach the texts and the authors from a theoretical point-of-view. While the majority of the authors are decidedly postcolonial as per the literary generic they belong to, even Toni Morrison's fiction is assimilated as part of the configuration with which the comparative study of the authors' work is dealt with in the present volume.

There are several glaring omissions in the volume, especially if we consider the absence of Alice Walker, Doris Lessing, Iris Murdoch, Zadie Smith, Kiran Desai, Jhumpa Lahiri, Angela Carter, Mahasweta Devi, Bapsi Sidhwa, Anita Desai or the numerous other equally significant authors of the genre we like to call here 'women's fiction'. An apologetic attempt is made at the end of this volume by introducing these authors, but a more prescriptive and necessary detailing is expected in a later, and possible, companion volume. As it stands, an exhaustive study of women's writing is not possible due largely to the immense variety and cornucopia of writing that has emerged of late. However, the current volume marks an (apologetic) attempt to chart the territories of existing women fiction writers, using a blend that highlights the possible varieties at our possession.

The first chapter is focused on Nobel laureate Toni Morrison's highly acclaimed first novel, *The Bluest Eye* (1970). The novel is noted for its narrative technique and its realistic portrayal of the conditions of a young black girl's growing up in times when oppression for the woman of colour came not only from racial considerations and issues but also economic and gender.

The issues which are covered in the chapter can also be found across Morrison's other works, namely her concern with the issues of religion, racism, and gender issues such as incest or incestuous rape or the inter and intra-gender paradigms that plague relationships across colour, caste, creed, religion, language and nationality. The essay is also an extensive study of the concept of the 'fourth face of God' which had also been discussed in Allen Alexander's essay but with the added perspective of the transnational and postcolonial theoretical scaffolding that underpins the essays in this volume.

The second chapter is dedicated to a close reading of the various issues that can be found in Margaret Atwood's novel, *Surfacing*. Atwood, a Booker winner, writes widely on environmental issues, also allowing the infusion of feminist interrogation of her interested areas. She is also a postcolonial author insofar as her conditioning as a Canadian author seeking emancipation from American neo-imperialism is concerned. The novel deals with multiplicities including the context of 'gaze', animality and perversion, colonialism of the globalised world by American hegemonic forces and environmental issues. The chapter is an attempt to capture these diverse areas of Atwood's investigation and argument through an analysis of the individual novel. Multiple theoretical thrusts can be found in the chapter, thus also acting as an exercise in theory-in-practice.

The 'Afterword' to the volume presented a unique dilemma to us—should we present an Afterword that tries to locate similarities in the various authors discussed or should we discuss their dissimilarities, or even their individual literary characteristics? However, the resolution was provided through the very lacuna in the present volume—the absence of multiple authors whom we would have liked to include. Therefore, the Afterword also acts as a glossary where we have written short biographical entries on important twentieth century women writers across nationalities. The short span of volume length allotted to the entries dissuades us from writing at length about each author but we have discussed thei salient features of their writings, their important works and any celebrated awards or prizes won by them. Much like the book, the list too seems inadequate to us at various times but should act as a precursor to a follow up volume rather than a full fledged glossary that could cover most or all reference work for the presently discussed genre.

Journals such as *Women's Writing* (Taylor and Francis) and *Contemporary Women's Writing* (Oxford) have provided a wider stage for interaction between the scholarly reader and the possibilities in the thus far isolated 'genre' of women's writing, consisting in part of fiction.

With volumes such as the present one and also multiple volumes being dedicated towards the reading of individual authors by renowned academicians, it is inevitable that the genre of women's writing is to be well developed not merely in practice but also in analysis in due time. The deficiency in substantial analyses of women's writing requires longer discussions than this, and the Afterword could possibly act as an induct towards a more significant volume with a wider spread of women fictioneers who may be analysed from a comparative and theoretical perspective replete with considerations of Poststructuralism, postcolonialism, postmodernism and the scaffolding of world literature in a globalised world.

Works Cited

Beauvoir, Simone de. *The Second Sex*, trans. H.M. Parshley. New York: Knopf, 1953. Print.

Chakraverty, Lalima. *Gender and Culture in the Works of Indian Subcontinent's Select Women Novelists*. New Delhi: Atlantic, 2012. Print.

Showalter, Elaine. "Feminist Criticism in the Wilderness." *Modern Criticism and Theory: A Reader*. Ed. David Lodge. New Delhi: Pearson, 2007. 325-348. Print.

Tharu, Susie and Lalita, K. *Women's Writing in India: 600 B.C. to the Present,* Vol. I. New Delhi: Oxford University Press, 1991. Print.

Tharu, Susie and Lalita, K. *Women's Writing in India: 600 B.C. to the Present,* Vol. II. New Delhi: Oxford University Press, 1993. Print.

TONI MORRISON'S *THE BLUEST EYE*: READING RELIGION, ETHICS AND AESTHETICS OF THE AFRICAN-AMERICAN WOMAN

Whether we generalise or codify Toni Morrison's writing as African-American women's fiction or feminist fiction or postmodern fiction, it remains a 'generic' ambiguity. Rather than such definitive signifiers, Toni Morrison's oeuvre of fiction is quite possibly best summed up in her own words, when she tells an interviewer:

> "I write for black women. We are not addressing the men, as some white female writers do. We are not attacking each other, as both black and white men do. Black women writers look at things in an unforgiving loving way. They are writing to repossess, rename, reown." [1]

This repossession and renaming is a process that *becomes* Morrison in a like manner as Alice Walker, Maya Angelou, Gloria Naylor or Toni Cade Bambara—enacting this identity is Morrison's fiction, as reformative and not static, or, to borrow from the French philosopher, Gilles Deleuze, *active*, not reactive. Morrison effectively "refute(s) the hierarchical order shaped by the concepts of centre and periphery and question the ideology on which the order is based" (Pal 2439) through her fiction, and also particularly in the novel under present consideration, *The Bluest Eye* (1970). While the apparent strand of postmodernity in Morrison's fiction is her accentuation of certain identifying characteristics of Afrocentrism, the celebration of *difference* is visible as well, as is the reliance on metanarratives. And although it has been stated that "exploring the complexity of Black female experience in white America," Morrison, in *The Bluest Eye* in particular, attempts to magnify and eventually "resolve the contradiction inherent in her African-American identity" (Ibid). Morrison's novels are an exploration of *blackness*—a blackness that includes the woman, the coloniality, the Postcoloniality, the enslavement, the prejudices, the denial of basics, of an identity, of suffrage and of opinion, the suppression of free will and rationality, of expression—of being "a Black woman in a white male hegemonic society" (Ibid).

One of the fundamental queries pursued in this essay—the question of religion and godhead—is also a contested area for Morrison, by extension of the Eurocentric values that such coded religion endorses. As Morrison states: "My work requires me to think about how free I can be as an African-American woman writer in my genderised, sexualised, wholly racialised world." [2] The questioning takes a hermeneutic, more than an epistemic, format—

11

the ordinance is on the emancipating from a European epistemology which privileges canonical religion, whiteness, and other *remedial* ancillaries whereas the blacks are marginalised and forcefully removed from the mainstream [3]. *The Bluest Eye*, an early novel, as well as one which brought considerable attention to Morrison, exposed the layers of impairment that this whiteness of the mainstream inflicted upon the minoritarian blackness. While interrogating the hegemonic formations that constructed micro-societies of each black existence Morrison also endorsed a questioning of religion—'the fourth face of God' as Allen Alexander's excellent essay [4] introduces to us as being innately and intricately absorbed within the narrative of the novel. Why the extensive suffering without any iota of salvation from the pre-condition of fallenness only on the part of the Black?—is a question that seems to emanate from Morrison's *The Bluest Eye*.

The 'double consciousness' which Morrison explores in *The Bluest Eye* is rooted in African-American existence—the inclusive exclusion of the community, on the basis of color, from the American dream and parallel experiences. The psychological fragmentation of the African-American individual facing such discrimination and exclusion is methodically explored by W E B Dubois:

> "[The] Negro is a sort of 7th son, born with a veil and gifted with second sight in this American world, a world which yields him no true self-consciousness, but only lets him see himself through the revelation of the other world. It is a peculiar sensation this double consciousness, this sense of always looking at one's self through the eyes of others, of measuring one's soul by the tape of a world that looks on in amused contempt and pity." [5]

This mirroring oneself through prejudiced eyes is a practice that the African-American individual, the sufferer, and especially the oppressed black woman has to undergo—*othering* the self continuously in order to locate the vantage point. The absent centre of whiteness and blue eyes is made the most desirable object, and its continued absence makes her own existence criminal and ugly for Pecola Breedlove, the protagonist of the novel. The American dream for this young African-American girl is to become the object of her fetish—a fair, or pure white woman, with blue eyes—symbols of Caucasian-ness that she is genetically devoid of. Perhaps the tradition of alienating the African origin person is also extensively responsible for the psychological evolution of Pecola in this manner, the justification of slave narratives by historians, politicians and philosophers including Hume, Kant and Hegel, and the development of eugenics as an exploration into the deficiencies of an entire racial community.

Before encroaching upon the domain of the 'fourth face of god', we shall explore some of the other relevant areas for considering the novel, including the fundamental concepts of African-American identity, blackness and the conception of beauty, and the representation of a psychological fragmentation that Morrison aptly induces with her exploratory, almost postmodern style of narrativising. Morrison's layered style of fiction makes it difficult to place within specific contexts without the possibility of overlapping ideas, but it is also this diversity that ensures her intense validity beyond the very society or culture she consciously affects in her novels, to a greater readership, presenting her personal critique of historiography through what Henry Louis gates refers to as "speakerly texts" [6].

The ideological and socio-normative policies of the dominant group are reinforced through the institutions that affect the regulations—education, mass or popular culture, healthcare, media, religion et al. And, by extension, it is the image of the dominant race or group that becomes a normative status for all subordinate social classes and racial groups—a viable and enviable non-being of whiteness, white-defined beauty and blue eyes which the protagonist of *The Bluest Eye* wishes to appropriate in and for herself. Patricia Hill Collins has identified the axis of beautification and the multiplicities involved in the 'Afrocentric' concept of beauty thus:

> "From an Afrocentric perspective, women's beauty is not based solely on physical criteria because mind, spirit, and body are not conceptualised as separate, oppositional spheres. Instead, all are central in aesthetic assessments of individuals and their creations. Beauty is functional in that it has not meaning independent of the group."
>
> (Collins 89)

And this holistic notion of beauty when corrupted by a hybrid sense of artificial beauty is "probably the most destructive idea in human history and thought" (Morrison 1999). Morrison's fiction is replete with a distinct atmosphere of a Black woman's survivalism in a scenario where she is shunned by white man's exclusivity and is also a victim of the rages of the African-American male, and where her psychology is the content to be dominated and transformed, as

"Indeed, the interests of the oppressors lie in changing the consciousness of the oppressed, not the situation which oppresses them . . . for the more the oppressed can be led to adapt to that situation, the more easily they can be dominated".

(Freire 47)

Beauty, or the contemporary cultural connotation of the concept of beauty, is a major site of conflict in *The Bluest Eye*, engendering the interrogation of broader and more varied discourses, as Ágnes Surányi remarks:

"A tragic story of child abuse, with race, gender and class mixed in, *The Bluest Eye* is concerned with racial self-loathing, the loss of identity, and shame. Even though the setting for the story is 1940–41 – the beginning of World War II for the United States – it is also "presentist" in concept, ideologically grounded in the 1960s when "Black is Beautiful" entered into the popular, if more militant, discourse. Setting out to write a story that she herself wanted to read, Morrison worried that this slogan of racial pride would be unable to dispel the long-term psychic effects of prejudices rooted in racialism and sexism."

(Surányi 11)

The popular culture phenomenon that had been rooted in Black consciousness was potent enough to transgress into the racial psyche as a permanent fixture. The icon-bearing impact of Hollywood culture, of the several consumer-centric industries that decided on the definition of beauty ensured it at the cost of a marginalised section that would be brutally cut off from that very segmentation of beauty. In *The Bluest Eye* the chronicling of this beauty locates the centre of this manufactured beauty in the white sections of the American populace, and the Blacks on the other end of this hegemony of appearance. The variations of the reception of this ideological 'beauty' are to be seen in Claudia's mutilation of the doll to find out the essence of the blue eyes that represent this notion of beauty, and in Pecola's ardent desire to become invisible, limb by limb, as an attempt to escape the squalor of her life, but her inability to get rid of the complexion of her eyes. "Like Ralph Ellison's *Invisible Man* her "ugly" black skin impedes any acknowledgment of the child within" (Surányi 12).

Pedagogy, adoption and adaptation are indeed the blunt instruments of the white society's domination over the African-Americans, as Morrison recounts. Strategic curriculum ensures the modelling of the young learner within the prescribed social normative of white society, as even the school primer testifies to:

14

"Here is the house. It is green and white. It has a red door. It is very pretty. Here is the family. Mother, Father, Dick and Jane live in the green-and-white house. They are very happy . . ."

(Morrison 1)

Going against the grain of humanism and enlightenment rationality as means of self-progress, education thus becomes a confinement that upholds stereotypes and prejudices without overt or violent means, rather through the propagation of an ideology. This ideology of preference is what Morrison directs her diatribe against, and she is conscious of the acquiescence that African-Americans showcase when encountering the effects of such ideological strategies. It is such false appropriation that leads to the eventual disintegration of the psychological makeup of Pecola: "Ontologically insecure, she is doomed to fragmentation. Her eventual retreat into insanity reveals her pathetic inability to cope with her hostile environment" (Pal 1994: 2440). However, this collapse of an African-American girl's identity does not cause Morrison to launch into an indictment against the vicissitudes of the dominant white class, but rather to ensure a balanced overview where she carefully examines the fault lines existing within the Black community as well, especially if we are to inspect the development of the character of Cholly Breedlove, Pecola's father, an individual who amply presents the vices of his racial masculinity or patriarchy with justification. Paternal rape has been a common signifier of the deterioration of Black society in America in such novels as Ralph Ellison's *Invisible Man* and Alice Walker's *The Color Purple* as well—always depicted as a taboo but ever present as a dreadful, and very real, spectre of Black associativeness.

Two values which definitively populate the fiction of Morrison, and especially *The Bluest Eye*, are the contexts of family and African-'Americanism'. Pecola is devoid of a stable and nurturing family structure, unlike Claudia, and is therefore always in a state of hapless ambiguity. The scaffolding of the family structure produces an ontological certainty which Pecola lacks, and longs for. Morrison affects her novels with the most poignant, poetic and aesthetically rendered scenes of mother-daughter interaction, and a similar scene in *The Bluest Eye* brings out the absent familial centre in Pecola—the scene where Claudia's sickness is met with a fretful mother. Although an incorrect usage within the current scenario of gender enquiries, Morrison's depicted sororities are wholesome and inclusive for themselves, preparing a strong bond that helps execute the most difficult personal decisions. Furthermore, Morrison does not merely have to contend with the question of Afrocentrism, that Alice Walker takes up radically and specifically, but has to advocate African cultural values in conjunction with her innate Americanism:

> "Whereas Alice Walker in her recent novels tends to take a radical Afrocentric feminist position, Morrison while advocating African cultural values is also conscious of the complexity of her situation as African and American and therefore explores the dynamics of cultural conflict."

> (Pal 2443)

Beyond the generic enquiries that may be directed to Morrison's *The Blest Eye* is the interrogation and presentation of religion in the novel. As Allen Alexander states:

> "Religious references, both from Western and African sources, abound in Toni Morrison's fiction, but nowhere are they more intriguing or perplexing than in *The Bluest Eye*. And of the many fascinating religious references in this novel, the most complex-and perhaps, therefore, the richest-are her representations of and allusions to God. In Morrison's fictional world, God's characteristics are not limited to those represented by the traditional Western notion of the Trinity: Father, Son, and Holy Ghost. Instead, God possesses a fourth face, one that is an explanation for all those things-the existence of evil, the suffering of the innocent and just-that seem so inexplicable in the face of a religious tradition that preaches the omnipotence of a benevolent God."

> (Alexander 293)

Morrison does not possess access to a specific or expressive Satan, and her only recourse is to deviate from the floating signifier and icon of a benevolent God and to present one who is hybridised by African folklore—a mischievous denizen of the heavens who discharges the duty of both pleasure and suffering. The hybridization affects in a Janus-headed mode—the African tradition of omni-emotive god/s affects Western models just as much as the Western models affect the African traditions involving multiplicities of God. "If *The Bluest Eye* can in any way be characterized as an initiation story, then a major portion of a character's initiation involves discovering the inadequacy of Western theological models for those who have been marginalized by the dominant white culture" (Ibid). The religious metaphors are not merely objectively located in the novel but also in the characters who equate Christianity with whiteness that they wish to appropriate or have already adapted to psychologically, and as an anti-Black equation. Characters ranging from Pauline Breedlove to Soaphead Church,

Geraldine and Mr. Yacobowski all attempt to negate Pecola's sense of an identifier religion, a distinction that she bears along with her fascination for whiteness and blue eyes. Religion, quasi-middle-class living, and an obliteration of Black psychological markers are ideological salvation for individuals who wish to escape the common fate of the Blackness of African-Americanism.

Curiously, the image of an African religious tradition is reinforced by Cholly Breedlove, as Allen Alexander recounts Morrison's depiction of the incident of Cholly's witnessing a 'God-like' white man. In his childhood, at a church picnic, "Cholly watches the father of a family raise a watermelon over his head to smash it on the ground and is impressed with the man's god-like stance, which he sees as the opposite of the unimpressive white image of God" (Alexander 1998: 294):

> "[A] nice old white man, with long white hair, flowing white beard, and little blue eyes that looked sad when people died and mean when they were bad".
>
> (Morrison 106)

Although this image of 'god-likeliness' impresses Cholly, he is reluctant to adopt it as a practice or ideology, and, at least for the time, embraces his African heritage. However, the lack and inadequacy which Cholly feels with regard to this *white-man's* religion is considered to be of paramount importance by Pauline who vehemently denies her African roots with the expectation of assimilation into a whiter mainstream, even if as a subordinate, but closer to the dominant ideological, social, cultural and racial group. However, this is in contrast to what the traditional religiosity of Africa is, and serves to convolute or unnecessarily pollute the benevolent practices, as God, in the African-influenced theological outlook is "neither threat nor rival" to humans, but

> "God is ... the very basis or ground of the creature's fullest possible self-realization ... Black religious experience ... is about being and becoming more human under God". [7]

But this becoming human, in Pauline's eyes, is the exclusive domain of the white man, the middle-class section of a race based on color who create the regulations in the most powerful democratically administered nation, and therefore not a possibility for Cholly to be a participant of.

Unlike the African tradition of god, where the divine figure is seen as immanent to the human or the mortal, Western theology views Godhead as distinct and transcendent to mortal existence, an "otherworldly presence who, despite Christ's role as redeemer or fallen humanity, regards human weakness, in the form of sin, as something disconnected from the divine" (Alexander 1998: 295). The Western canon of God ascribes a stoic and patriarchal position for him, dictating terms which are to be observed by all and sundry, a role which is taken up by an immense section of the white populace. God in the African tradition, on the contrary, is a friendly figure who possesses a sense of humour and a streak of fallibility—proportionately human. Cholly attempts to interpret and integrate these characteristics into himself, but fails because he has long been dominated by the Western, chiefly white canon, and his reading of the African tradition of Godhead is awry and inflected with attempts and kindness along with the fallacies of white divinity. On the other hand, Morrison reads into the character of Pauline as inappropriate and self-defeating—a woman who privileges white religion over her own traditional religious location. Morrison believes that God is not homogeneous or unilateral with the conditioning of humanity, and that is the reason why she introduces, or rather endorses the 'fourth face' of God—not expressly a Black face but one that does not shun blackness as inferior. Western theology has largely confined the notion of God into a benevolent transcendental signifier without any participation in the tragedies of humans, but African tradition, showing God as a willing or inactive participant or audience in the tragedies of humans makes 'Him' palpable within human and general cultural narratives—even the tragedy of blue eyes, of the violation of Pecola and all its allied histories is thus accountable in Morrison's hybridization of Christianity.

The fourth face is finally developed when Cholly's impression of the white man breaking the watermelon at the church picnic is accounted, reinforcing the heritage of African tradition of God:

> "It must be the devil who looks like that—holding the world in his hands, ready to dash it to the ground and spill the red guts so niggers could eat the sweet, warm insides. If the devil did look like that, Cholly preferred him. He never felt anything thinking about God, but just the idea of the devil excited him. And how the strong black devil was blotting out the sun and getting ready to split open the world."
>
> (Morrison 107)

"The image that Cholly relishes is one that embraces the fourth face, one that portrays God as much more than the pallid, antiseptic God envisioned by white society. Cholly's God is dynamic, complex, unpredictable, exciting, dangerous" [8] (Alexander 1998: 298-9). Cholly permits the idea of a God who can inflict damages and is destructive; an idea which might unsettle white cultural dimensions, but is inherently adjusted within the African amalgam or assemblage of God.

Pecola's position in this false religiosity is particularly precarious—she is alienated on a primary level by her dissociation from any sense of beauty as affected by her color and secondly by the abhorrence which her physical appearance is usually met with. She is unable to adapt to the Western theological Christianity and is also distanced from an African heritage as Pauline's cultural and psychological insistence or reinforcements have negated the possibility of her ever happily associating with her own color:

> "Pecola has become so disconnected from her heritage that her movement toward insanity is instead an indictment of the white cultural framework that has become her guidepost for living."

> (Alexander 299)

However, Pecola, like all of Morrison's range of *reactive* characters, does not take this tragedy in acquiescence or powerless acceptance. She resists through an active imagination, to which a Deleuzian 'line of flight' [9] is provided by her violation, her rape by her own father, but is continued with a sense of the very tragedy because it needs to be "dealt with, survived, outwitted, triumphed over" (Morrison 1999: 118). Even her eventual, and conclusive, insanity-ridden image of acceptance of the tragedy meted to her is an act of resistance that resounds with the African tradition of the 'fourth face' of God—an act of resistance or rebellion against the patriarch of the Western theological God resulted in the expulsion of angels from heaven, but Pecola falls without even the opportunity of resistance. If any truth can be extracted, it is so that Pecola subscribed not only to Western theology, but also its allied practices as centrally discursive of white culture, and yet, she is met with a brutal fate. Although Cholly's rape of her is a physical transgression, Pecola is most affected by Soaphead Church's indictments against her appearance. Soaphead is an accomplished molester of young girls, but that is not what he subjects Pecola to. Rather, he psychologically assaults her where she is weakest and destroys her possibilities of becoming, robbing her of her true sense of identity. And it is in and through Soaphead that Morrison presents her diatribe against Western theological tradition—making him the representative of every vice that the white man's Christianity is capable of. But there are amends—the schizophrenic beliefs of Soaphead himself resonates those of Cholly or, to a lesser extent, Pecola—the convoluted hybridization of a white God, immanent devil, and the fourth face of the traditional African god. Amidst all the obfuscatory search for the forth face of God in the novel it is finally revealed that the coveted transcendental existed, from the inception, in Claudia's elusive, almost Ouroboros-like narrative, which "is in itself a reflection of the image that is central to her heritage: the fourth face of God" (Alexander 302).

"In Morrison's work, history emerges as a nurturing cultural foundation from the dialogic interaction . . . [She] establishes a point of intersection between the different voices in a commitment to recover and rewrite . . ." (Vendrame 684). While on the other hand, tragedy in *The Bluest Eye* is also classically treated as immanent to existence, of to borrow from Gilles Deleuze, transcendentally empiricist—existing within itself, i.e., life, and not beyond or exterior to it:

> "Morrison's novels reveal that the idea of 'Fate' is one often mobilized to obscure historical causes and effect, to which human agency is key. The novelist's politically-motivated refutation of 'Fate' constitutes a modification of the conventional classical tragic condition."

> (Roynon 213)

Rather than a Nietzschean or Deleuzian *amor fati* [10], however, what we find in its place is an *'abhor' fati* given the intense dislike to biological and racial formations. Fate for the racially oppressed is a pre-given condition that furthers the cause of the 'racial superiors' in the oppression, democratic suppression and psychological repression—a notion which Morrison counters with her militant fiction. What the reader obtains through the semi-arboreal expansions of Pecola or Cholly in the novel are not multiplicities of racial avengement and reverse historiography but the prevailing singularities of identity and a subversion and de-sublimation of the crises characterizing the racial 'condition'. To ethically limit or aesthetically sensitivize Morrison's fiction for the purposes of a general canonical absorption or inclusiveness would surmount to an impossibility, and so is a preliminarily historical understudy inadequate in defining the parameters of her writing; but it is for a literary signification of genres that one might refer to Morrison's first novel, i.e. *The Bluest Eye*, it suffices to say that the novel is significant not only in its revisitation of the black historiography and aesthetics, but also a revalidation of the possibilities that an emancipated black feminist/feminine writing could entail. It is of substantial import also that Morrison's revisionary tactic provides the later ground for more militant and postmodern authors such as Alice Walker and Zadie Smith to perform similar acts of textual, contextual and extratextual subversions of the given historical roles.

Notes

[1] Cited in Nellie McKay, *Critical Essays on Toni Morrison*, G K Hall and Co, Boston, Massachusetts, 1988, p. 46. The question of identity and representation are of paramount importance in Morrison, as her exploration is also centred along the *decentering* of a fixed, pre-Abolition idea of African-Americanness.

[2] Cited from Toni Morrison, *Playing in the Dark: Whiteness and Literary Imagination*, Picador, London, 1992. The notable difference in Morrison is from other Black women writers, including Alice Walker. Although the presence of the masculine is intrinsic, Morrison's treatment of the transgressive male is ancillary to the other realities of her fiction.

[3] The conceptual framework of 'mainstream' is ideological—it depends on several, often discursive, factors, which, for Morrison, most often accrued of the Eurocentric contraptions of a strictly white mainstream standardised society.

[4] Allen Alexander, "The Fourth Face: The Image of God in Toni Morrison's *The Bluest Eye*", in *African American Review*, Vol. 32, No. 2 (Summer, 1998), pp. 293-303. The essay discusses the possibility of a 'fourth face' of divinity, or godhead, whereby the canonical, and parochially Eurocentric Trinity is rendered obsolete as the concerned divine authorities merely seem occupied with infliction of punishment.

[5] Cited from W E B Dubois, *Dark Water, Voices from Within the Veil*, A M S Press, New York, 1969, p. 45. The pseudo-ontological assemblage presents a socio-historical, cultural, and meta-religious commentary that emancipates this Black-ness from the folds of White *supremacy*.

[6] In Henry Louis Gates, Jr's definition, "speakerly texts" are those in which the rhetorical strategy is designed to represent 'an oral literary tradition'.

[7] Major J. Jones, *The Color of God*, Mercer UP, Macon, p. 22, cited in Allen Alexander (ref. Bibliography), p. 295.

[8] See Jacqueline de Weever, "The Inverted World of Toni Morrison's *The Bluest Eye* and *Sula*," *CLA Journal* 22 (1979): 402-14 for a discussion involving the pattern of inversion, of contrasting images of black and white, as seen in *The Bluest Eye*.

[9] 'Lines of flight', in the terminology of Deleuze and Guattari refer to assembled disruptions—events which fracture other incidents—and evidenced here particularly by Pecola's placid imagination and fantasies being violently disrupted by the trauma and transgression of rape.

[10] Love for *what is*.

Works Cited

Alexander, Allen. "The Fourth Face: The Image of God in Toni Morrison's *The Bluest Eye*", in Harold Bloom (Ed.) *Bloom's Modern Critical Interpretations: Toni Morrison's* The Bluest Eye, pp. 111-124. New York: Infobase, 2007. Print.

Amian, Katrin. *Rethinking Postmodernism(s): Charles S. Peirce and the Pragmatist Negotiations of Thomas Pynchon, Toni Morrison, and Jonathan Safran Foer*. Amsterdam and New York: Rodopi, 2008. Print.

Bloom, Harold (Ed.). *Bloom's Modern Critical Views: Toni Morrison*. Philadelphia: Chelsea House, 2005. Print.

Bloom, Harold (Ed.). *Bloom's Modern Critical Interpretations: Toni Morrison's* The Bluest Eye. New York: Infobase, 2007. Print.

Burrows, Victoria. *Whiteness and Trauma: The Mother-Daughter Knot in the Fiction of Jean Rhys, Jamaica Kincaid and Toni Morrison*. Hampshire and New York: Palgrave Macmillan, 2004. Print.

Collins, Patricia Hill. *Black Feminist Thought: Knowledge, Consciousness and the Politics of Empowerment*. Boston: Unwin Hyman, 1990. Print.

Collins, Patricia Hill. "Defining Black Feminist Thought", in Carole R. McCann and Seung-kyung Kim (Eds.) *Feminist Theory Reader: Local and Global Perspectives*, pp. 341-356. New York: Routledge, 2012. Print.

Duvall, John N. *The Identifying Fictions of Toni Morrison: Modernist Authenticity and Postmodern Blackness*. Hampshire: Palgrave, 2000. Print.

Erickson, Daniel. *Ghosts, Metaphor, and History in Toni Morrison's* Beloved *and Gabriel García Márquez's* One Hundred Years of Solitude. New York and Hampshire: Palgrave Macmillan, 2009. Print.

Freire, Paulo. *Pedagogy of the Oppressed.* London: Pelican Books, 1972. Print.

King, Lovalerie and Lynn Orilla Scott (Eds.). *James Baldwin and Toni Morrison: Comparative Critical and Theoretical Essays*. Hampshire and New York: Palgrave Macmillan, 2006. Print.

Miner, Madonne M. "Lady No Longer Sings the Blues: Rape, Madness, and Silence in *The Bluest Eye*, in Harold Bloom (Ed.) *Bloom's Modern Critical Views: Toni Morrison*, pp. 7-22. Philadelphia: Chelsea House, 2005. Print.

Morrison, Toni. *The Bluest Eye.* London: Vintage, 1999. Print.

Morrison, Toni. *Playing in the Dark: Whiteness and Literary Imagination.* London: Picador, 1992. Print.

Pal, Sunanda. "From Periphery to Centre: Toni Morrison's Self Affirming Fiction", in *Economic and Political Weekly*, Vol. 29, No. 37, Sept. 1994, p. 2439-2443. Print.

Roynon, Tessa. *Toni Morrison and the Classical Tradition: Transforming American Culture.* Oxford: Oxford University Press, 2013. Print.

Russell, Danielle. *Between the Angle and the Curve: Mapping Gender, Race, Space, and Identity in Willa Cather and Toni Morrison.* New York and Oxon: Routledge, 2006. Print.

Ryan, Judylyn S. "Language and narrative technique in Toni Morrison's novels", in Justine Tally (Ed.) *The Cambridge Companion to Toni Morrison*, pp. 151-161. Cambridge: Cambridge University Press, 2007. Print.

Samuels, Robert. *Writing Prejudices: The Psychoanalysis and Pedagogy of Discrimination from Shakespeare to Toni Morrison.* New York, Albany: State University of New York Press, 2001. Print.

Smith, Valerie. *Toni Morrison: Writing the Moral Imagination.* Sussex: Wiley-Blackwell, 2012. Print.

Surányi, Ágnes. *"The Bluest Eye* and *Sula*: black female experience from childhood to womanhood", in Justine Tally (Ed.) *The Cambridge Companion to Toni Morrison,* pp. 11-25. Cambridge: Cambridge University Press, 2007. Print.

Tally, Justine (Ed.). *The Cambridge Companion to Toni Morrison.* Cambridge: Cambridge University Press, 2007. Print.

Vendrame, Alessandra. "Toni Morrison: A Faulknerian Novelist ", in *Amerikastudien / American Studies*, Vol.42, No. 4, Special Issue on 'William Faulkner: German Responses, 1997, pp. 679-684. Print.

Wong, Shelley. "Transgression as Poesis in *The Bluest Eye*", in Harold Bloom (Ed.) *Bloom's Modern Critical Interpretations: Toni Morrison's* The Bluest Eye, pp. 53-66. New York: Infobase, 2007. Print.

NATURE, ONTOLOGY AND FEMININITY:
A STUDY OF MARGARET ATWOOD'S *SURFACING*

"Whether the wilderness is

real or not

depends on who lives there."

Atwood[1]

Margaret Atwood's *Surfacing* (1972)[2] is generally viewed as the novel which is most closely associated or attached to her poetry, with which it shares "a considerable thematic and stylistic territory" (Grace 97). There is a considerable difference in Atwood's previous novels, particularly *The Edible Woman*, and *Surfacing* with its "terse, laconic style and consciously poetic imagery and metaphor, more subtly employed" (Tolan 35) than the former novel. There is a simultaneous transformation in *Surfacing* that Atwood affects her writing with which showcases the stylistic shift that attempts to comprehend an expansive scenario of how Atwood's dialogue transmogrifies through several dissonant political events and concerns. The novel also possesses a theoretical foresight which has helped it in occupying privileged positions in contemporary feminist and ecocritical debates, interrogating the intense role-play to which 'minor'[3] segments of the society were exposed to, with "the unnamed protagonist (shrugging) off human identity altogether by the end of the novel, preferring to seek the resolution to her problems by refusing to speak altogether" (Macpherson 30)—thus issuing interpretations which stretch from the historical, the ecofeminist, sequentially as per ecological criticism, deep ecology, mainstream feminism, as well as a postcolonial approach, to one involving classical psychoanalysis, as well as a Deleuzoguattarian exploration of the 'becoming-woman' ; or, to quote Fiona Tolan, in a comparative trajectory of evolution from Atwood's previous novel:

> "*Surfacing* continues and develops *The Edible Woman*'s preoccupation with the female protagonist and her alteration from social expectations, but introduces issues of ecology, nationalism, spirituality and ancestry to Atwood's canon of political focus."
>
> (Tolan 35)

From another critical context Sharon Rose Wilson has referred to *Surfacing* as "an anti-novel or anti-romance like Samuel Beckett's *Molloy*" (Wilson 178) on multiple occasions, stating: "Both Beckett and Atwood write prose which may be hard to distinguish from poetry or may have affinities to visual art, and both excel at parody. Significantly, *both* subvert conventions of genre, plot, structure, usage, and punctuation in shaping texts which question their own existence" (Wilson 54).

The development of the character of the protagonist in *Surfacing* is a curious one that draws from her memories or the lack thereof, her silences, awkward social being and becoming, and her resolution to attempt inclusion into a more general and accepted canon. As Roberta White states: "The nameless narrator of *Surfacing*, sometimes referred to as the Surfacer, lacks self-knowledge; in fact, through much of the book she suffers from a self-imposed state of amnesia in which she has suppressed the facts of her own life story" (White 161). A victim of circumstances and of a monstrously callous married lover, the narrator of *Surfacing* has too meagre, and at times too idealistic, a grasp of reality to achieve success as an artist. She is a commercial artist and book illustrator, having been goaded onto that path by her first lover, who was also her art teacher: "For a while I was going to be a real artist; he thought that was cute but misguided, he said I should study something I'd be able to use because there has never been any important women artists" (Atwood 49). When she embarks on her intensely allegorical journey into the wilderness of Quebec in search of her lost father, the narrator takes along her watercolours and acrylics in order to illustrate a book of fairy tales, but her fingers soon "grow stiff and feel arthritic" (White 161). She cannot perform the sort of "imitative, insincere art" (Ibid) that is expected of and even demanded from her—images of women as idealized princesses. Furthermore, even her publisher forbids her use of hot or bright colours, even for a tale of the Golden Phoenix; fire must somehow be painted with a cool tone, an act that in no way leads to the incitement of overt behaviour. It is not surprising that the narrator's hopes for a career in art are aborted: "forced into commercial art because of gender stereotypes, she discovers that the commercial field promotes those same stereotypes" (Ibid).

Several details of *Surfacing* anticipate another novel by Atwood, *Cat's Eye,* written seventeen years later: "the background of the narrator's family, her childhood in the wilderness, the disastrous affair with her art teacher, and the book illustrations" (White 162). But *Surfacing* is not about the narrator's art, commercial or otherwise; it is about submersion, immersion and self-discovery, about becoming rather than the 'being as a woman' of the protagonist. Atwood calls the *Surfacing* a ghost story: "the narrator's denial of her own history—the fact that her lover has forced her to have an abortion—leads her to create in her own mind a false history in which she is married and has abandoned her child" (Ibid). The narrator's most fervidly expressive moments of sanity and self-control occur when she is floating alone or with her companions in a canoe on the lake searching for her father: "It's like moving on air, nothing beneath holding us up; suspended, we drift home" (Atwood 64). She navigates well in the wilderness and feels most at home suspended in its beauty, enterprising a melancholy 'within' nature rather than merely 'in' it. "Although it seems for a time that her increasingly intense mistrust of words and language will lead her more fully into a world of visual expression—maps, drawings, photographs—the narrator eventually burns all of her own and her family's records, including her artwork, paints and tools, along with her childhood drawings and scrapbooks in order to 'clear a space' in which she can descend for a time into, literally, an animal existence, devoid of language or civility" (Ibid). These events occur after she mystically "sees" the ghosts of both her parents—although this may be interpreted as a schizophrenic or hallucinatory event or experience as well. Another element that is intensively projected in the novel could, at least terminologically, be placed in context with Hegel's 'end of art' thesis as well as Barthes' concept of the 'death of the author':

> "Although several of the elements of this story can be found in other novels about women artists—the sensation of suspension above water, the longing to enter into the mysteries of purely visual experience, and even the return of the ghosts—it is obvious that this narrator's art is a dead end."

> (Ibid)

The unnamed protagonist is, rather, cut off from her feelings and the people that surround her — estranged from everyone — though this only becomes apparent much later, since the reader initially trusts her and does not notice the absence of a name for some time. We learn that the woman is travelling with her boyfriend Joe, her best friend Anna, and Anna's husband David with the sole intention to look for the narrator's father and leave at the earliest possible instance, but instead the two couples agree to spend two nights in the family cabin on the lake. This later extends to a week as the men decide to fish as a means of escape from the bustle of their regular city lives. "These seven days are metaphorically significant, in that the narrator's world isn't created, but essentially dismantled, during the week" (Macpherson 31)—an auto-biblical reference that only serves further in the negation of binary moral paradigms and their obsolescence. When she encounters drawings made by her father, she is convinced of his insanity and of a diabolical plot involving the couples: "indeed, though not named as such, the father figure becomes, in her imagination, a sort of *wendigo* figure, or mythical creature who is said to watch and feed on family" (Ibid). With a carefully measured symmetry, Joe and David too metaphorically seem to feed on those around them, especially the female characters/bodies, particularly in relation to an amateur film they are making, titled *Random Samples*. This film is a montage of shots of tourist spots, ironically filmed; shots of a dead heron[5] strung up as if on a crucifix—left, they believe, by invasive American fishermen—and the exploitation of Anna, who is, at one point, forced to strip for the camera (Jeremy Hawthorn implements 'theories of gaze' to this visual violence, as cited in the endnotes)[6]. At a higher level of metaphor, those who are destructive become, in the narrator's mind, Americans—invaders or colonisers. All that is bad is ejected from the narrator and assigned to this other nationality – so much so that the narrator ends up assigning the category American even to those who insist they are Canadian:

> "It doesn't matter what country they're from, my head said, they're still Americans, they're what's in store for us, what we're turning into. They spread themselves like a virus, they get into the brain and take over the cells and the cells change from inside and the ones that have the disease can't tell the difference. Like the late show sci-fi movies, creatures from outer space, body snatchers injecting themselves into you dispossessing your brain, their eyes blank eggshells behind the dark glasses. If you look like them and talk like them and think like them then you are them, I was saying, you speak their language, a language is everything you do."
>
> (Atwood 123)

Atwood's focus on language in *Surfacing* has been explored critically from as early as 1976, when Nancy Bjerring published an article in the *Queen's Quarterly*; and a focus on language works quite well, despite the silences or 'silent presences' of the narrator and her inability to communicate.

The spectre of duplicity is threaded through the narrative of *Surfacing* in, for example, the way in which of the characters relate to each other. One particular example focuses on Anna, who expresses her duplicity through her relationship with her husband: "she and David present—at first—the image of a loving couple who work hard at their marriage. They 'tease' each other frequently, which the narrator first reads as a sign of their closeness and only later recognizes as passively aggressive behaviour. She gets up early to put on make-up, noting that her husband does not like to see her without it—but she subsequently claims that he does not know she wears it" (Macpherson 32). The narrator notes, "I glimpse the subterfuge this must involve, or is it devotion" (Atwood 38). The transition from 'subterfuge' to 'devotion' is suspect, but aptly reflects a reiteration of 'gaze' (Hawthorn 2006), where the devotion too is a party to the panoptic patriarch. "The reader understands—if the narrator does not—that subterfuge better characterizes their fraught relationship, yet it is also telling that the narrator *consciously* reworks the words she uses" (Macpherson 32). This suggests an active attempt to change or alter significantly the appearance. Anna claims that her marriage works because she made an 'emotional commitment' (Atwood 41), though later that commitment is eventually revealed as one of hate. Although Anna is represented as deluded in her marriage, in fact, she faces reality more than the narrator. When she sees the narrator's paintings of princesses, she remarks, "They shouldn't let kids have stuff like that" (Atwood 52) since she knows the lie of 'happily ever after' will forever disappoint them as a result of such renditions. When Anna eventually discloses David's serial unfaithfulness, the narrator's response is telling: "I was sorry she'd told me; I still wanted to believe that what they called a good marriage had remained possible, for some" (Atwood 93). The narrator misses the obvious signs of their unhappiness, "from the fact that Anna is not consulted about important plans, to David's sexist comments and Anna's sexually provocative behaviour as a result, to the fact that Anna is forced to strip as part of *Random Samples*" (Macpherson 33). She sees one particular instance unilaterally when it is abundantly clear that another image is available. Put simply, the novel acts as a palimpsestic[7] text—a text that is layered over with meanings that erase and disrupt the picture that the reader receives.

This disruptive 'texture' of Atwood's creation is at multiple points as assemblage in itself, accessing "the sight of the narrator as it unfolds multiple *becomings* and platitudes" (Macpherson 34). Upon encountering the corpse of her father, unable to cope with the destructive collapse of her identity, her "carefully constructed and self-manipulative realities," (Ibid) she reverts to childhood behaviour, a self-serving and defensive fundamental escapism—"The only defence was flight, invisibility" (Atwood 129). The protagonist's attempts to conceive a child with Joe, despite their estrangement, is fraught with internal conflicts and an animalistic conditioning in her—opting for the process in the wilderness, under moonlight, like the mating of animals, functional. It is contradictory because she intends to leave the human world behind. It is, besides, also of consequence that the narrator opts for the seventh day to be the day of their departure—"the Christian symbolism having been sustained throughout the novel" (Macpherson 34). However, setting aside the associations and metaphors of myths, legends and religions, the reference could be drawn to a consideration of the attempt at conception as a re-populating of the new world, as attested further by the narrator's lovemaking with Joe outside the confines of the old world symbol—the cabin, a human habitation. The narrator becomes, in Joan Larkin's words, "unhuman" (Larkin 50), and it is at the discretion of the reader to decide "whether she is mad, whether she is a 'creative non-victim' or whether she is simply escaping again instead of confronting the reality of her situation" (Macpherson 34). She is referred to as "inhuman" (Atwood 148) by her companions for her failure to communicate, but it is perhaps the narrator's transformation from a societal *becoming*-woman to an immanent *becoming-animal*, minoritarian, and intrinsically possible. She refuses to pretend to be civilized, and admits, "From any rational point of view I am absurd; but there are no longer any rational points of view" (Atwood 163).

The narrator's acting out by dumping the exploitative film *Random Samples* is a manifestation of this latter becoming:

> "What follows is a descent into the animal world, into possible madness and into a period where the narrator communes with the ghosts of her parents. In her animal state, she avoids certain areas as taboo, refuses to use human implements (in fact she destroys some) and sheds her clothing. She also becomes entirely filthy, refusing to groom herself (and by this point, she has no other animal or human to help her do so; indeed, grooming has been seen quite negatively in its association with Anna's false face)."

> (Macpherson 34-5)

This 'naturalisation' of the narrator is not a romantic or pastoral beautification but rather the regression of the woman into a primitive state of further becoming, not being static in her position even at that stage, responding against idyllic overviews of nature, patriarchy and society, as J. Brooks Bouson remarks:

> "When the Surfacer ... becomes transformed into the 'natural woman,' she both rebels against the masculinist mindset that maps and delimits the world and enacts her secret desire to escape from the contained, domestic sphere of femininity. But although she escapes masculine logic and domestic confinement in her merger with nature, and although the text insistently privileges nature over civilization, the Surfacer's transformation into the 'natural woman' is still unsettling."

> (Bouson 58)

It is indeed difficult to read into the transformation, or transmogrification, of the narrator, as Atwood relies on images rather than logic to move the narrative forward, and, as Danielle Schaub suggest, that rather than "defining the self in relation with the vast physical landscape," the novel defines "landscape as internalised geographies of the self" (Schaub 220). The image of her encounter with her father, in a hallucinating state, in the shape of a wendigo, is particularly obfuscating, and often perplexing with its verbal grandeur: "It does not approve of me or disapprove of me, it tells me it has nothing to tell me, only the fact of itself" (Atwood 181). The 'fact of itself', however, leads her to reconsider her opted for existence, and, imagining a commune with her parents—"I saw them and they spoke to me, in the other language" (Atwood 182)—she finds herself reverting, or, specifically in the previous context of becoming-animal, regressing into her human nature. She thereafter makes her famous claim about refusing to be a victim, and about taking responsibility—a statement which is as much humanist as it is feminist (or ecofeminist), positing a rational and moral grounding within the discourses of society. The novel reaches its conclusion, with Joe's return, and the narrator tenses towards him, but does not resist his arrival by an escape—she does not respond yet to the calling of her name, but there now exists a potential of the same. As Heidi S. Macpherson remarks:

> "This ending, one of potential but not final movement, works well, in that it shows the lengths she has yet to travel in order to inhabit fully her humanity. Atwood's narrative endings – where resolutions are rarely offered, though images are stark and suggestive—work to unsettle the reader and keep the reader actively engaged in the story, long after the last page has been read."

> (Macpherson 35)

In contrast to the all encompassing narrative of her previous novel, *The Edible Woman*, Atwood's *Surfacing* presents an archaeology of "both a time and a person on the point of serious rupture" (Palumbo 23). Language plays an intimate role in the development and 'becoming' of the protagonist as early 1970s Anglophone Canada and its relationships with the United States and francophone Canada are presented in parallel to the story of the nameless narrator, "a woman on the verge of complete breakdown due to an unvoiced, but real, grief" (Ibid). The different categories and narrative genres in which this novel has been analyzed or interpreted by critics—as ghost story, family story, anatomy of a breakdown—all highlight the layering of histories and cultures in the novel, paving way for the inclusion of strategies that anticipate a utopia of themes. In the novel, the narrator drives north from

Toronto with her partner and another couple to the isolated lake in Quebec where she was brought up by stubbornly rationalist, yet idealistically innocent, parents. The narrator's father has disappeared, which prompts her first visit north in nine years—a return from a self-imposed exile. During the trip, the narrator is put at unease by the way in which almost the entire region has "changed, yet not changed, as time seems to her to have congealed; meanwhile, the reader is discomfited by the narrator's mysterious evasions and absences" (Ibid). The narrator simultaneously affirms her doubled existence, "now we're on my home ground, foreign territory" (Atwood 11), and denies it, describing a childhood split between the city and the wilderness, and an affectless present, of mere existence in shallow concepts of society. The truth of the narrator's memories is hidden beneath feverish and convoluted polarities. Her more ambiguously happy childhood is hidden behind the preternaturally idyllic one she describes, while a failed affair and an abortion lie beneath her disturbingly violent descriptions of marriage and childbirth. An unvoiced, but lurking, anxiety is the source of the narrator's need to order things in neat binaries: for her, leeches are "good" or "bad," humans are bad, animals good[4], and the mind and the body are two separate things—a careful reader could find analytical resonance with Deleuze's classification of the animal. The narrator's eventual, and seemingly unavoidable, breakdown comes in her attempt to throw off all influences of the "human" and "American," and become "natural"; since this flight from the human depends on there being rigid separations between the natural and human—giving the human increased importance even in the process of evading it—it is doomed to failure. The authentic, as Atwood shows, is found in a synthesis of the two, and not at either pole of natural or human exclusively.

The narrator's realization that the victim/victor binary must be transcended is the key to her integrating all aspects of her personal fragmented history:

> "This above all, to refuse to be a victim. Unless I can do that I can do nothing. I have to recant, give up the old belief that I am powerless and because of it nothing I can do will ever hurt anyone. A lie which was always more disastrous than the truth would have been."

> (Atwood 191)

As the narrator acts out, and resolves, her own emotional rupture, the narrative depicts Quebec and Canada shifting into a more clearly self-defined identity that attempts to break out of the impulsive and oppressive shadow of America. "Behind the characters' apocalyptic rhetoric describing the landscape and Canadian culture is a very real sense of Canada's growing unease with American hegemony and a corresponding sense of nationalism that itself is working away from victim/victor games" (Palumbo 24). The narrator and Atwood herself are concerned about the extensive impact of American hegemony on the Canadian social spheres which they are susceptible to, as well as the effects of neo-colonialism that penetrate the layers of being and consciousness of gender, culture, nature and mode of life. This hegemony is not merely counter-productive for the Canadian populace culturally but also erases all traces of a past, even a pre-Caucasian (pre-colonial) indigenous past. The narrator's breaking apart from social conventions is not affected only on a personal scale but also on in a larger schematic which connects all divergent features of her existence. What this modified form of colonialism negates is the modicum of her ontological identity, which she promptly replaces with a post-ontological and post-phenomenological sense of becoming— becoming-woman and becoming-animal by turns.

Surfacing is a novel with a wide spectrum that is inclusive of multiple concerns, and not all of them involving a specific Canadian context. Atwood's writing is thoroughly Canadian, but her concerns are also evolutionary in that they concern and revolve around multiplicities—the contexts of gender and gender-related debates are valid even at present, as are the ecological concerns and the context of global American hegemony, and each of these debates and concerns have morphed perfectly into a poststructural or postmodern form. Thus, the novel was not just contexted and contextual at the time of its publication, but has also proven itself to be a complex, yet desirable, assemblage of constant becoming. The ambiguity of its finale is testament to the morph-ability of the novel, but most importantly, of its varying *surfaces*:

> "An ecofeminist novel that revisited (the romantic pastoral cycle of retreat and return), to see how it might work in feminist and environmentalist terms, was Margaret Atwood's *Surfacing*. The novel ends with the woman protagonist poised, perhaps about to return from her pastoral retreat, perhaps about to return from her pastoral retreat, perhaps committed to it as permanent transformation. . . Such a disappearance into nature would be a refusal to complete the pastoral cycle of retreat and return. . .: a withdrawal from communication with modernity."

> (Kerridge 540-41)

The reader surfaces, at the end of the novel, into a cognizance of realities of ecology, neocolonialism, being and becoming, animalism and other faculties which coerce this previously unaffected reader into a confrontation with this so far 'preserved' self: "The unnamed female narrator in the novel, too, has to 'surface' from the false views of herself that she has internalized, at the end of the novel turning mirrors around so that she cannot see herself and forcing herself to confront who *she* thinks she is" (Hawthorn 516). The unnamed, but responsive, reader too has no particular surface at the end of the novel, but a confrontation of multiple and conflicting philosophies which in turn aid in a readerly becoming akin to the becoming of the unnamed protagonist of *Surfacing*.

The processes that the reader encounters through the narratorial vision in *Surfacing* are profoundly impacted by the effects of a 'post-colonial' status of historical as well as geographical orientations. Unlike the narratives of homogenous colonial conditioning in the works that is to be discussed later, *Surfacing* is the only work where the spectre of colonialism is monadic—the past of twin colonial appropriations causing a linguistic binary and the contemporariness of the neo-colonial significance that is concurrent to the author's sociohistorical understanding of her present. Therefore, in view of the present assessment, the becomings that the narrator experiences are relative to the proportion of colonial experiences that are native to the postcolonial woman who is undergoing a multiplicity of identity formations to allow her emancipation from colonial as well as patriarchal domination. Atwood's politicization of the identity-quest of womanhood is an important aspect of writing from the woman's experiences, and can perhaps be best framed theoretically with Gerda Lerner's remark which sums up Atwood's stance *vis-á-vis* the question of women's writing being representative of women's identity:

> "It is important to understand that 'woman's culture' is not and should not be seen as a subculture. It is hardly possible for the majority to live in a subculture […]. Women live their social existence within the general culture and, whenever they are confined by patriarchal restraint or segregation into separateness (which always has subordination as its purpose), they transform their restraint into complementarity (asserting the importance of woman's function, even its 'superiority') and redefine it. Thus, women live a duality—as members of the general culture and as partakers of women's culture."

> (Lerner 52)

Notes

[1] Atwood, Margaret. "Further Arrivals", in Margaret Atwood and Charles Pachter, *The Journals of Susanna Moodie*. Boston and New York: Houghton Mifflin, 1997 [1970].

[2] Citations of the novel will be furnished from the 2009 re-issue of the novel (London: Virago). For details, refer to 'works cited'.

[3] The concepts of 'minor/ity' and 'becoming-woman' here are drawn from Deleuze and Guattari and will be elaborated referentially in subsequent passages. Also notable is the concept of 'becoming-animal' that Deleuze and Guattari describe as the process of 'assemblage' that the minoritarian animal has to undergo in its stages of becoming in order to obtain a temporal being, and could specifically be applicable to the transmogrification of the unnamed protagonist of the novel.

[4] The Deleuzian connection that helps in linking this 'animality' of *Surfacing* with his: "Deleuze admits his fascination with spiders, ticks, and fleas; their environment is limited in terms of affects yet it constitutes *a* world. Most probably with Von Uexküll (1957) in mind, he reveals his fascination for the power (*puissance*) of these worlds confined to a small number of stimuli. Animal territories are another fascination for Deleuze. Claiming a territory, he says, is where art began" (Beaulieu 70).

[5] The eocritical/ecological importance of the 'dead heron' is immense; the death of an 'indigenous' animal represents the invasion of this very selfhood of Canada by brash Americans who cut down trees, destroy the ecology and disrupt the 'flow' of life.

[6] "In Atwood's novel the violence congealed into the ways in which men see women is painstakingly and painfully revealed. In the most shocking scene in the novel, one of the two male characters, David . . . forces his wife Anna to strip naked so he can film her, in front of the female narrator and her male friend. But the threat of violence is always behind how Anna presents herself to David—and, as Berger (1972) suggests is the case for many women—to herself. . . Watching has been the prelude to violence for so long that it easily slips over into actual violence" (Hawthorn 516).

[7] In art terms, a palimpsest is a parchment that has been partially erased and then painted or drawn over with another image. As the piece of art ages, the first image can bleed through, creating a new, hybrid image. Atwood's use of the palimpsest image is formally appropriate, given the fact that the main character and her lover are both artists.

Works Cited

Atwood, Margaret. *Wilderness Tips*. New York: Anchor, 1991. Print.

Atwood, Margaret. "Cryogenics: A Symposium." *When the Wild Comes Leaping up: Personal Encounters With Nature*. Ed. David Suzuki. New South Wales: Allen & Unwin, 2002. 143-8. Print.

Atwood, Margaret. *Surfacing.*1970. London: Virago, 2009. Print.

Beaulieu, Alain. "The Status of Animality in Deleuze's Thought." *Journal for Critical Animal Studies*, Vol. IX, Issue 1/2, 2011, pp. 69-88. Print.

Bloom, Harold (Ed.). *Bloom's Modern Critical Views: Margaret Atwood*. New York: Infobase, 2009. Print.

Bouson, J. Brooks. *Brutal Choreographies: Oppositional Strategies and Narrative Design in the Novels of Margaret Atwood*. Amherst: University of Massachusetts Press, 1993. Print.

Christ, Carol P. "Margaret Atwood: The Surfacing of Women's Spiritual Quest and Vision." in *Signs*, Vol. 2, No. 2 (Winter, 1976), pp. 316-330. Print.

Garrard, Greg. *Ecocriticism*. New York and London: Routledge, 2004. Print.

Goldblatt, Patricia F. "Reconstructing Margaret Atwood's Protagonists." in *World literature Today*, Vol. 73, No. 2 (Spring, 1999), pp. 275-282. Print.

Grace, Sherrill. *Violent Identity: A Study of Margaret Atwood*, edited by Ken Norris. Montreal: Véhicule Press, 1980. Print.

Hawthorn, Jeremy. "Theories of the Gaze." *Literary Theory and Criticism: An Oxford Guide*. Ed. Patricia Waugh. Oxford: Oxford University Press, 2006. 508-18. Print.

Hengen, Shannon. "Margaret Atwood and environmentalism." *The Cambridge Companion to Margaret Atwood*. Ed. Coral Ann Howells. Cambridge: Cambridge University Press, 2006. 72-85. Print.

Howells, Coral Ann (Ed.). *The Cambridge Companion to Margaret Atwood*. Cambridge: Cambridge University Press, 2006. Print.

Kerridge, Richard. " Environmentalism and Ecocriticism." *Literary Theory and Criticism: An Oxford Guide*. Ed. Patricia Waugh. Oxford: Oxford University Press, 2006. 530-43. Print.

Larkin, Joan. "Soul Survivor." *Critical Essays on Margaret Atwood*. Ed. Judith McCombs. Boston: G.K. Hall, 1988. 48-52. Print.

Lerner, Gerda. *The Majority Finds Its Past: Placing Women in History*. New York: Oxford University Press, 1979. Print.

Macpherson, Heidi Slettedahl. *The Cambridge Introduction to Margaret Atwood*. Cambridge: Cambridge University Press, 2010. Print.

Palumbo, Alice M. "On the Border: Margaret Atwood's Novels." *Bloom's Modern Critical Views: Margaret Atwood*. Ed. Harold Bloom. New York: Infobase, 2009. 21-34. Print.

Ridout, Alice. "Temporality and Margaret Atwood." *Bloom's Modern Critical Views: Margaret Atwood*. Ed. Harold Bloom. New York: Infobase, 2009. 35-58. Print.

Rigney, Barbara Hill. "Alias Atwood: Narrative Games and Gender Politics." *Bloom's Modern Critical Views: Margaret Atwood*. Ed. Harold Bloom. New York: Infobase, 2009. 59-66. Print.

Schaub, Danielle. "'I am a Place': Internalised Landscape and Female Subjectivity in Margaret Atwood's *Surfacing*." *Mapping Canadian Cultural Space: Essays on Canadian Literature*. Ed. Danielle Schaub. Jerusalem: The Hebrew University Magnes Press, 2000. 91-106. Print.

Suzuki, David (Ed.). *When the Wild Comes Leaping up: Personal Encounters With Nature*. New South Wales: Allen & Unwin, 2002. Print.

Tolan, Fiona. *Margaret Atwood: Feminism and Fiction*. New York and Amsterdam: Rodopi, 2007. Print.

Waugh, Patricia (Ed.). *Literary Theory and Criticism: An Oxford Guide*. Oxford: Oxford University Press, 2006. Print.

White, Roberta. "Northern Light: Margaret Atwood's *Cat's Eye*." *Bloom's Modern Critical Views: Margaret Atwood*. Ed. Harold Bloom. New York: Infobase, 2009. 159-80. Print.

Wilson, Sharon Rose. *Margaret Atwood's Fairy-Tale Sexual Politics*. Jackson, MS and Toronto: University Press of Mississippi and ECW Press, 1993. Print.

Wilson, Sharon Rose. "Blindness and survival in Margaret Atwood's major novels." *The Cambridge Companion to Margaret Atwood*. Ed. Coral Ann Howells. Cambridge: Cambridge University Press, 2006. 176-190. Print.

DOWN LENNY'S MEMORY LANE:
PORTRAIT OF AN AGONISED FEMALE'S PARTITION HISTORY IN BAPSI SIDHWA'S *ICE CANDY MAN*

"I have grey eyes in this lifetime and they are wide open as I am severed from my mother's womb. The futility of tears is for those who have not, as I have, rolled the dice a few times."

— Shauna Singh Baldwin

(Prologue to *What the Body Remembers* p.1)

This tendency to 'roll' the 'dice' and to see the 'other side' of the coin called 'history' has made the sub-continental women writers radical. Among them the Pakistani woman novelist Bapsi Sidhwa is the prominent one to write about the theme of partition, more especially on the theme of violence either domestic or national done more particularly on the women. Her exclusive indulgence on the feministic approach throughout her books made it clear that the traumatic experience of partition by the women of that time and after that affected her thought process and a vast literary body has been the result of that. It has been assumed for a long time that the sub-continental Muslim women could not express their voices within them — they usually mutilated and suppressed them under their 'borkha' which is the sign and symbol of inequality and injustice. Even then her *Ice-Candy-Man* (1988) and later published as *Cracking India* (1991) strives to enter into a world which was the devastation of women 'body' and 'psyche' through the non-human process of 'cracking' a country into pieces. And this 'cracking' was not only creating boundaries among nations but also 'cracking' the woman 'body' in terms of its 'psychology and soul' — feelings and desires. In other words this process of 'cracking' was done on the 'body' and blood of women. Peculiarly enough, but truth is truth, their bodies can walled up the line between Indian sub-continent. Her own childhood memory is the impelling instigator for her to travel through the memory lane of Lenny:

"The novel reflects my own experience as a Parsi living in Lahore in the 1940's. It reflects how the position of the Parsis was difficult at a time when there was so much animosity between Hindus, Muslims and Sikhs in Western Punjab. Second, how does one feel as a Parsi, growing up in a society with different religious communities living in close proximity with each other before partition, changing to genocidal hatred between them in post-partition period. I remember there used to be regular fights over the issue in our house. Once or twice, visitors even came to blows with each other during a particularly tense argument over politics. Even today what do Indians and Pakistanis talk about when they meet? They discuss politics and do so vehemently."

(Bhalla 226)

The novel while revealing the memory of Lenny, the eight years old crippled girl who ruminated the memories which were drawn upon a socio-cultural background unveiling the 'position' of women in there. Through Lenny Sidhwa created a female universe obliterated repeatedly by the reductive and restrictive forces of patriarchy and colonialism. Thus, her world became an endless chain of fragmented memories. In the very first chapter of the novel the reference to this 'compressive' attitude of the society was revealed in Lenny's words:

"My world is compressed . . . my child's mind is blocked by the gloom emanating from the wire mesh screening the oblong ventilation slits (of Salvation Army Wall). I feel such sadness for the dumb creature I imagine lurking behind the wall. I know it is dumb because I have listened to its silence, my ear to the wall[. . .] ."

(*Ice-Candy-Man* 1)

So this suppression and marginalisation of woman came up in this novel at two different levels — the pre-partition and the partition situations. In the beginning of the novel Lenny described the sensuous attractive capability of the Ayah Shanta for her physical abortiveness. She became the centre of attraction for the persons of different communities—the Fallatis Hotel cook, the Government House gardener, the butcher, the compactly muscled-head and body masseur and the Ice Candy Man and the object of their 'eye-rape':

"Up and down, they look at her. Stub-handed twisted beggars and dusty old beggars on crutches drop their poses and stare at her with hard, alert eyes. Holy men masked in piety shove aside their pretences to ogle her with lust."

(*Ice-Candy-Man* 3)

This indicates at the very lustrous attitude of the male domain that could not look at a woman with a soft-equal-eye and as a human being rather as a delicious 'object to devour on and tear apart. In the similar vein, in the peaceful pre-partition pluralistic Lahore Lenny because of her lameness was deprived of the formal education. Col. Bharucha identifies her physical deformity with her femaleness to deprive her of a proper education:

"According to the doctor ... She is doing fine without school ... Don't pressure her ... her nerves could be affected. She doesn't need to become a professor. She will marry, have children, lead a carefree, happy life. No need to strain her with studies and exams, he advises, thereby sealing her fate."

(Ice-Candy-Man 15)

This injustice was the outcome from a society where woman was 'positioned' into a compartment devoid of light and 'exit'.

But this 'positioning' of woman was subtle and 'neutral' because as a partition woman novelist she did not belong to either of the 'communities of discord'—Hindus and Muslim. She was born in a Parsee family. Regarding this 'de-familiar' position of Sidhwa Subhash Chandra in his critical work, *Bapsi Sidhwa's Ice Candy Man: A Feminist Perspective* comments:

"Ice Candy Man commands attention and admiration on several counts. It is the second novel by a woman writer (the first being *Sunlight on a Broken Column* by Attia Hosain) dealing with the theme of partition of India, but it is the first by a non-partisan writer, as Bapsi Sidhwa being a Parsee does not belong to either of the two communities which perpetrated mayhem on each other...."

(Chandra 118)

This 'detatchment' from her 'subject' made her to look at the political event of Partition from an different angle from the traditional troupe of writing and which made her committed towards a social group and led her to record the voices of marginalised as evident in her interview with David Montenegro:

"As a writer, as a human being, one just does not tolerate injustice, I felt whatever little I could do to correct an injustice I would like to do. I have just let facts speak for themselves, and through my research I found out what the facts were."

(Montenegro 36)

The novel's gynocritical view of reality is casted from a feminine perspective through the feminine experience of their 'body' and 'psyche'. The transformative attitude of the socio-cultural setting forced the women characters of this novel—Lenny, the Ayah, Godmother, Lenny's mother et al to assume 'new roles'. Lenny, her mother, Godmother, and Shanta exhibited that transcendence of roles and position. Shanta was a working girl in a family where her position was that of a 'subordinate'—a nourisher and caretaker of a crippled girl. But gradually for the political partition she was thrashed into a new paradigm. The political change of the scenario, namely the partition, forcefully enslaved her into an unfamiliar position. She was violently abducted by her Muslim suitor Ice Candy Man and the grotesque sight impels the agonised cry from within the bodies long buried:

> "They drag Ayah out. They drag her by her arms stretched taut, and her bare feet —
> that want to move backwards — are forced forward instead. Her lips are drawn away
> from her teeth, and the resisting curve of her throat opens her mouth like the dead
> child's screamless mouth. Her violet sari slips off her shoulder, and her breasts strain
> at her sari-blouse stretching the cloth so that the white stitching at the seams shows. A
> sleeve tears under her arm. The men drag her in grotesque strides to the cart and their
> harsh hands, supporting her with careless intimacy, lift her into it. Four men stand
> pressed against her, propping her body upright, their lips stretched in triumphant
> grimaces."

(*Ice-Candy-Man* 183)

Ice Candy Man later married her and renamed her as Mumtaz and compelled her to sell her 'body' as a prostitute in Hira Mandi. What is new in this book is that a 'patriarchal tool' (Ice Candy Man) was the possessor of the body of the girl and at the same time 'dispossessed' the body of the same person. In this respect it is evident that patriarchy uses the body of a woman by engaging the 'ideological' tools of false hope, love and affection and; at last pressure as the successful means for its own good shake.

This 'Double Dealing' of the patriarchy in Ice Candy Man raises another question in this novel. At the end of the novel we encounter Ice Candy Man in a new shape and in a new way. He transformed himself into a poet and when Mumtaz was taken away from him and kept in the House, he used to keep flower on the high walls and recited poems of love for his love for the girl:

> "Each morning I awaken now to the fragrance of flowers flung over the garden wall at
> dawn by Ice-Candy-Man. The courtyard of the Recovered Women's Camp too is
> strewn with petals; and sometimes with the added glitter of cheap candy wrapped in
> cellophane."

(*Ice-Candy-Man* 277)

Now it is the question posed here did he really love the girl? Then what made him to abduct the girl and led her into the pathetic prostitution? Or was it simply the vengeance towards another community? And if it is so, then why should the vengeance raised against a particular community (Hindus) fall on the girl (Shanta)? From the day first, it has been assumed that the women are the easy prey for the men. Ice Candy Man was not an exception of that. He exploited the 'body' which he himself craved once and later fall in 'love' with that 'ruined-impure' body. And his love was ringing along the gullies of Lahore:

> "Why did you make a home in my heart?
> Inhabit it. Both the house and I are desolate.
> Am I a thief that your watchman stops me?
> Tell him, I know this man. He is my fate.
> Don't betray me, beloved, I'm God-intoxicated!
> I'll wrap myself about you; I'm mystically mad."
>
> *(Ice-Candy-Man* 276-277)

Looking at the point above it is evident that Sidhwa subverts the romantic patriarchal concept of 'love' and 'being loved'. Here the 'unnatural' love of Ice Candy Man was subverted and took by the novelist to a different level—the level of 'insanity'. This is only a fragmental peeping through the 'black-hole'—Partition—we don't know how many Shantas were loved in the same way by the Ice Candy Men. Surely, it is the greatest jolt the book has for the patriarchal norms. This thwarted love clearly should be termed as 'cruel love'. But somehow, for his cruelty towards Shanta's 'body and soul' he was not forgiven into the history of partition. And this violent act of his gave birth to a striking and strange position of the Shantas.

But Sidhwa did not stop after subverting the traditional notion of love, she, then, turned towards the makers of history spreading satiric and slanting rays from a 'neutal' Parsee view point on the apocalyptic event of 1947. The 'heroic' and 'sublime' figure of Gandhi was altered in a comical tone of Lenny:

> "Gandhijee visits Lahore. I'm surprised he exists. I almost thought he was a mystic figure [...] He is knitting. Sitting cross-legged on the marble floor of a palatial veranda, he is surrounded by women. He is small, dark, shrivelled, old. He looks just like Hari, our gardener, except he had a disgruntled, disgusted and irritable look, and no one'd dare pull off his dhoti! He wears only the loin-cloth and his black and thin torso is naked."
>
> *(Ice-Candy-Man* 85)

So this subversion of the great historical figures in the novel is done through a feminist perspective—Sidhwa like all the other sub-continental woman writers blamed them for bringing a disastrous end upon the women. No matter what history says but these writers believe that the 'blood of body' and 'honour' of the women drew the boundaries among these nations. This ridicule of Gandhi in Ice Candy Man is viewed by Rahul Sapra as:

> "Unlike most of the Indian historians who credit Gandhi for single-handedly ousting the British from India, in *Ice-Candy-Man* Sidhwa reduces him to the role of an eccentric dietician."

(Sapra 201)

So what is that striking stage? The following conversation between Lenny and Godmother casted a very different light on the position of Shanta and Hamida,another maid of Lenny's household:

> "What a fallen woman?" I ask godmother…
> "Hamida (the second Ayah) was kidnapped by the Sikhs",
> Says godmother seriously… When that happens sometimes,
> The husband – or his family won't take her back."
> "Why? It isn't her fault she was kidnapped."
> "Some folk feel that way — they can't stand their woman
> being touched by other men."

(*Ice-Candy-Man* 215)

Not only Hamida or Shanta but also thousands of other women got into a strange position due to their 'impure' bodies which were touched by the men from other castes. In this respect the words of Ritu Menon and Kamla Bhasin are worth citing:

> "tattooing and branding the body with "Pakistan, Zindabad!" or "Hindustan, Zindabd!" not only mark the woman for life, they never allow her (or her family and community) the possibility of forgetting her humiliation. In the deep horror of its continuous and forever present recall of brutality, this particular violation has few parallels. In the context of partition, it engraved the division of India into India and Pakistan on the women of both religious communities in a way that they became the respective countries, indelibly imprinted by Other."

(Menon & Bhasin 43)

This traumatic situation for the women led the women to form another group— either they went to some religious place for the life time to sacrifices their desire to God or Allah. Again the idea of Stasa Zajovic gives the relevance glimpses to the same situation from a different context. While analysing the mass rape of women in Bosnia-Herzegovina, she says that —

> "as a result of rape the female womb becomes occupied territory. In Serbo-Croat the term 'cleansing' is popularly used for abortion, but abortion takes on a particular political significance in circumstances such as these. The idea of polluting and cleansing applies especially to women's bodies."

(Zajovic 36)

Thus, their identities were in a continual state of construction and reconstruction.

This is nothing but 'playing the patriarchy for enjoyment. Partition in this respect is not only the partition of the subcontinent but also the partition of the women body from its 'honour'. This 'dissection' has been merely overlooked as 'violence'. But this is not only a violence but also one kind of 'cruel enjoyment' on the part of the patriarchy not merely to 'posses' the body of women but to exploit and demolish the 'possibility' of emotions and feelings within them. And there came the term 'honourably dead' as pointed out by Ritu Menon and Kamla Bhasin :

> "These deaths were an instance of when, to acquiesce is not to consent, and to submit is not necessarily to agree. Notions of shame and honour are so ingrained and have been internalised so successfully by men and women, both, that a death which has been forced onto a woman may quite easily be considered a "willing sacrifice" even by women themselves."

(Menon & Bhasin 46)

Thus, their existence is at a serious stake. They were not only sexually abused but also their 'sexuality' was abused to construct a patriarchal tool of violence — "honourably dead" — a process through which they became bodily 'other' and sexually they were also the 'other'. The Ayah who was cherished by so many suitors for her body and sexuality, but at last her 'body' which was already an 'other' thing turned into another shape of 'otherness' — a "prostitutes' body" — not suitable for particular but for everybody or nobody.

Sidhwa ploted the novel by the innocent eyes of the two non-political narrators — Lenny and Ranna, a little boy of Pir Pindo village whom Lenny met while she visited that village. He escaped the brutality and violence done by the Shikhs to their village and the mouthed-gap description of it took fifteen pages in Sidhwa's book. In her visits to the village of Pir Pindo with their house-hold cook Imam Din Lenny saw the peaceful coexistence between the two communities. The Muslims of Pir Pindo and the Sikhs from the neighbouring village of Dera Tek Singh sit together and share their concern over the deteriorating communal situation and the outbreak of hostilities in the cities. The Muslim *chaudhary* of Pir Pindo tells Imam Din:

> "Our relationships with the Hindus are bound by strong ties. The city folk can afford to fight ... we can't. We are dependent on each other: bound by our toil; by Mandi prices set by the Banyas—they're our common enemy—those city Hindus. To us villagers, what does it matter if a peasant is a Hindu, or a Muslim, or a Sikh?"

> *(Ice-Candy-Man* 56)

But the Sikh villagers, despite their goodwill, fail to protect the Muslim brothers from the marauding bands of the Akalis who pounce on Pir Pindo and other Muslim villages to massacre the males, and rape the girls and women. Sidhwa showed both Muslims and Sikhs indulging in violence, yet the Muslims appeared pale beside the Sikhs in their atrocities. Sidhwa describes the mass murder of Muslims in Pir Pindo as Ranna saw it:

> "He felt a blow cleave the back of his head and the warm flow of blood. Ranna fell just inside the door on a tangled pile of unrecognisable bodies. Someone fell on him, drenching him in blood. Every time his eyes open the world appears to them to be floating in blood. From the direction of the mosque come the intolerable shrieks and wails of women. It seems to him that a woman in sobbing just outside their countryard: great anguished sobs—and at intervals she screams: 'You'll kill me! *Hai Allah* ... Y' all will kill me!"

> *(Ice-Candy-Man* 201-202)

The violators almost did to women what Sudhir Kakar termed as the process of "desexualisation" with a grave socio-political intention:

> "Amputating her breasts at once desexualises a woman and negates her as wife and mother; no longer a nurturer (if she survives, that is) she remains a permanently inauspicious figure, almost as undesirable as a barren woman...the amputation of breasts incorporate the (the more or less conscious) wish to wipe the enemy off the face of the earth by eliminating the means of reproduction and nurturing."

> (Kakar, 37)

In *Ice-Candy-Man,* religion was manipulated as a tool to play the patriarchy on the women in the vacuum of partition. The two communities Hindu and Muslim were fighting and killing one another for nothing or for the 'imaginary lines'. But they never thought the women as the 'rival' to contest with rather a very simple 'body' to play the 'virile dance' on. And it was evident in the character of Ayah through whose eyes Lenny saw the world. But what happened to them was not merely partition provoked but an already well-established socio-religious phenomenon. Their becoming 'second sex' was clear in the course of the events. When Lenny was growing up gradually she found her position of being the 'other'. Her cousin touched even the private parts of her body thinking her physically 'subordinate'. She was the 'other'(cripple) which made her body even more 'luring' and 'cheap' to the dominant male attention. Thus Lenny is clearly a 'shadow' of the Ayah only waiting to succeed the sequence of long line tolerating all pain and oppression without a word expressed and thus getting into a 'silence' from where their deep-long-buried voices can never be penetrated and revived. This formation clearly evokes the critical thinkers like Gayatri Chakravorty Spivak utter the agonised words:

> "The subaltern cannot speak. There is no virtue in global laundry lists with 'woman' as a pious item. Representation has not withered away. The female intellectual as intellectual has a circumscribed task which she must not disown with a flourish."
>
> (Spivak 313)

Again, as per Spivak's notion of representation, there arises a question— who would represent that voice? They could speak only to their own self and own confederates but no to others. The Ayah at last whispered to Godmother in the dirty cottage of Hira Mandi that she did not want to stay with The Ice Candy Man but told to nobody else about this:

> "Ayah's face with a demurely lowered lids and tinsel dust, blooms like a dusky rose in Godmother's hands. The rouge and glitter highlight the sweet contours of her features. She looks achingly lovely: as when she gazed at Masseur and inwardly glowed. But the illusion is dispelled the moment she opens her eyes — not timorously like a bride, but frenziedly, starkly — and says: 'I want to go to my family'. Her voice is harsh, gruff: as if someone has mutilated her vocal cords."
>
> (*Ice-Candy-Man* 261)

It clearly proves that the oppression and pain of a woman heart can only be opened at the presence of the other oppressed who could feel and who could hear the cry of their agony, but not the people (Ice-Candy-Man) who is doing and conducting the oppression from the above — the 'centre'.

Although a striking voice in the realm of feminist criticism, Sidhwa's passive negotiation with the brutal patriarchy was sometimes discernible in the voice of Godmother when she consoled the Ayah listening to her pathetic condition:

> "That was fated, daughter. It can't be undone. But it can be forgiven...worse tilings are forgiven. Life goes on and the business of living buries the debris of our past. Hurt, happiness... all fate impartially...to make way for fresh joy and new sorrow. That is the way of life."
>
> (*Ice-Candy-Man* 262)

'Forgive' and 'forgiveness' are words found only in the fictive dictionary of women. But this forgiveness is the 'negotiation' with patriarchy which turns their position into a loophole and they turn themselves into a negotiable position. Or through this 'sharing' of the agony with the ears of the same clan was the sign of 'building the wild'—the crescent area of the model presented by the Oxford anthropologist Shirley and Edwin Ardener and where remain exclusively the feelings of women:

> "Women constitute a 'muted group', the boundaries of whose culture and reality overlap, but are not wholly contained by, the 'dominant (male) group'; there is also a crescent which is outside the dominant boundary and therefore wild."
>
> (Ardener 3)

Even then Sidhwa is different from the other partition novelists. For instance, in Khushwant Singh's A Train to Pakistan Juggut, the heroic and moral centre of the novel had the physical sharing with Nooran who said:

> "That is all you want. And you get it. You are just a peasant. Always wanting to sow your seed. Even if the world were going to hell you would want to do that. Even when guns are being fired in the village. Wouldn't you?"
>
> (*A Train to Pakistan* 15)

Here Nooran's position is secondary and a mere receiver of the men 'semen' and the 'object of sex'. But in case of Sidhwa, she did not let the patriarchy play the postulates over any women character so freely in the novel. Lenny, for example, did not allow her cousin to play the game of chess with her and she protested in her own way:

> "But having only the two hands to do all this with he can't pull them down because galvanised to action I grab them up and jab him with my elbows and knees; and turning and twisting, with my toes and hills."
>
> (Ice-Candy-Man 231)

Thus, from the margin in the male partition chronicler the woman novelists like Bapsi Sidhwa tried to posit the women into the moral centre of the novel—which is radically not the centre but the symbolic centre. This kind of searching and shifting from the margin to the centre is evident in another two woman novelists — Manju Kapoor from India and Taslima Nasreen from Bangladesh. In this enigma, Ice Candy Man becomes a feminist text in the true sense of the term, significantly striving to bring to the 'centre-stage' the female protagonists — Lenny and the Ayah and at last, felt a sigh of relief:

> "Until, one morning, when I sniff the air and miss the fragrance, and run in consternation to the kitchen, I am told that Ayah, at last, has gone to her family in Amritsar... And Ice-Candy-Man, too, disappears across the Wagah border into India."
>
> (Ice-Candy-Man 277)

Works Cited

Ardener, Edwin. "Belief and Problem of Women." *Perceiving Women.* Ed. Shirley Ardener. London: Hammond World, 1982. Print.

Bhalla, Alok. *Partition Dialogues.* New Delhi: Oxford UP, 2006. Print.

Chandra, Subhash. "Bapsi Sidhwa's *Ice Candy Man*: A Feminist Perspective." *Feminism and Literature.* Ed. Veena Noble Dass. New Delhi: Prestige, 1995. Print.

Kakar, Sudhir, *The ColourS of Violence.* New Delhi: Penguin, 2000. Print.

Menon, Ritu and Kamla Bhasin. *Borders and Boundaries: Women in India's Partition.* New Delhi: Kali for Women, 1998. Print.

Montenegro, David and Bapsi Sidhwa. "Interview by David Montenegro." *Points of Departure: International Writers on Writing and Politics*. Michigan: University of Michigan Press, 1989. 25-55. Print.

Sapra, Rahul. "A Postcolonial Appraisal of Sidhwa's Fiction." *Bapsi Sidhwa's* Ice Candy Man*: A Reader's Companion*. Ed. Rashmi Gaur. New Delhi: Asian Book Club, 2004. 197-209. Print.

Sidhwa, Bapsi. *Ice-Candy-Man*. New Delhi: Penguin, 1989. Print.

Singh, Khushwant, *Train to Pakistan*. New Delhi: Penguin, 2009. Print.

Singh Baldwin, Shauna. *What the Body Remembers*. New Delhi: Rupa, 2011. Print.

Spivak, Gayatri Chakravorty. "Can the Subaltern Speak?" *Marxism and the Interpretation of Culture*. Ed. Cary Nelson and Lawrence Grossberg. Chicago: University of Illinois Press, 1988. 271-313. Print.

Zajovic, Stasa. "Women and Ethnic Cleansing." *Women Against Fundamentalism*, No.5, 1994, Vol. 1 (London) 35-59. Trans. Cynthia Cockburn.

BREAKING THE BARRIER OF SILENCE:
A STUDY OF MANJU KAPUR'S *DIFFICULT DAUGHTERS* AND SUNANDA
SIKDAR'S *DAYAMEER KATHA*

I do not wish them (women) to have power over men; but over themselves.

— Mary Woolstonecraft

True to this to make "room of one's own" from the "double colonial subjugation" and to raise their "suppressed" voices, the women had to pass through and to take resort to a large bitter canvas. In her study of the *Image of Women in Literature*, Mary Ann Fergusson writes, "One peculiarity of the image of women through the history is that social stereotypes have been reinforced by archetypes" (4). It is a tradition from the time immemorial that women were painted as "a mother, a wife, a mistress or an object of attraction and their roles have been defined in relationship to male counter-part. Depiction of women as achievers or leaders has been comparatively few" (ix). But in spite of the barriers and boundaries, some suppressed voices like that of Virmati of Manja Kapur's *Difficult Daughters* and Daya in Sunanda Sikder's *Dayamayeer Katha* get the force and power to break those barriers imposed on them and, eventually their silent voices get proper articulation.

Difficult Daughters recounts the story of Virmati, a young woman born in Amritsar into an austere Panjabi family who did not want to live her mother's life which revolved around domesticity, marriage and child bearing. She was the eldest of the nine children of Kasturi and — and she became the second mother the younger brothers and sisters tolerating a lot of pain and suffering. Literally she was being taught to conform to the rulesand regulations of a woman – the barrier set by painful patriarchy. But she did no longer want to see the world through the "glass" placed for her in her solitary confinement, she had her dreams — dreams to transgress the boundary and to peep through the window and break the glass into pieces. She was influenced by the words of her rebel and liberated cousin Shankuntala who fought against the family and went to Lahore to study in Lahore Government College. She became independent of the imposed patriarchy on her and to set a path of her own. From her later visits to her house Virmati was influenced and dreamt about breaking the barriers of painful patriarchy.

Nevertheless, the patriarchal expectation from her family did not stop at that point and it is evident in her own words:

My family tells me they are doing this for my good. I feel, since I have caused them so much grief, why don't they just let me go away and never see me again. God will provide – there are things I can do. When I suggested this they got very angry. They want nothing from me but an agreement to marry.

(Kapur 100)

This agonised "desire" to "go away" from the construction of the feminine has been harshly subdued and suppressed by the patriarchal constructive politics for the very sake of its own and particularly own "interest"; and the ultimate direction towards the metaphysics is evident in her taking resort to God as a provider and saviour which delineates the helplessness and "despaired submission" to another dominating politics. In the mean time she was in love with the Oxford returned married Prof. Harish. On the other side a groom was chosen for her by her family and she knew from her experience that her family could not sense her feeling of inner heart and her mental turmoil—nobody could listen to her "voice," and thus, engraving a deeper irony for the lifelong Indian tradition of getting the "daughters" married off without paying any heed to their liking and disliking. Instead of voicing her own desire, she remained silent putting up with the oppression of her family because of the scandal of her illicit love relationship with the professor. And that "silence" led her to do the attempt of killing herself—suicide and gradually turning to be the "difficult daughter" to the family.

As Tennyson's the Lady of Shalott, disavowing the "curse" upon her, emerged into a new word from the lonely and solitary tower: "Down she came and found a boat/ Beneath a willow left afloat", Virmati also, rebelled against her family as well as her mother's expectation, who believed:

There is time in the cycle of life for everything. If you will fully ignore it like this, what will happen to you? A woman without her own home and family is a woman without moorings.

(Kapur 111)

Thus, Virmati wanted to go beyond of the boundaries set by the principles of patriarchy, leaving aside the "anxiety of influence" created by her mother and got admitted into the Lahore College where she like her *behnji* Shakuntala could—"travel," "entertain" herself, "read," "drink" and "merry." This educating herself in the 1930s and 1940's breaking the "golden maxims" certainly represents Virmati as the spirit of Indian *new woman* which refers to the women who were swayed away by the educational surge that came upon in the first

52

half of the twentieth century and made them liberated from the domestic house-hold and set foot on the global arena of "womanhood" with their assertion of individuality.

But now the question arises here is that how far did she succeed? As Sheema Malik pointed out, "She failed to transcend her underlying need for love and emotional dependence," (135) and she lost the strength of her "voice" because her feeling for the professor was genuine and she did not want to sacrifice the bond of love for anything not even the pressure heaped on her by her family. But she was a mere girl then with the colourful dreams around her and her soft mind got shattered eventually resulting in losing the strength of her voice and is submerged into the deep gulf of barrier. She was vacillating between the demands of her heart and her yearning to be a part of the political movement of the time – the movement of empowering the women entity as did by the historical figures like Sarojini Naidu and Mrinalini Sen whom she set as her ideals in the novel. She failed pathetically succumbing to the professor's implorations .She yielded to temptations of the body and finally "aborted" the new life within her womb feeling the august pain silently because she found herself locked in new prisons even as she broke old ones. As Ida recounts Virmati's experience so as to give her "silenced" voice an proper articulation:

> That was all she wanted to do. Forget, forget, forget, forget. She felt a deep emptiness inside her, which she construed as yearning for the Professor. Oh, how she longed to meet him, to throw herself on his chest, babble out her story, feel his love and sympathy, his regret that he wasn't there pouring over her in a great tidal wave that would cleanse her of all guilt and sorrow!
>
> (Kapur 173)

The happiest and the attractive period in Virmati's life is that which she spent as the Head Mistress of a girl's school in Nahan, a small Himalayan state. She almost attained the autonomy over her life, which she had craved all along and eventually discovers her own space to live but she failed to restrain herself from succumbing to the demands of the relationship which she knew was doomed from beginning, but did not have the heart to deny. To quote Dora Sales Salvador:

> In *Difficult Daughters* we *do not* listen to Virmati's voice. She could not speak out, being certainly situated at the juncture of two oppressions: colonialism and patriarchy. What we have is her daughter's reconstruction and representation. (358)

Despite the shock and disapproval of both families the Professor eventually married her but Virmati's married life was a sheer disaster. She was ostracized by her famil, and forced compete for her share of her husband's love along with her first wife, Ganga. Virmati was forced to compromise and adjust in order to adapt herself into her husband's family and eventually died an insignificant death.

Sunanda Sikdar in her *Dayamayeer Katha* recounts the story of a barely twelve years old girl, Dayamoyee who watches with bewilderment as her village, Dighpait begins to change because of the historical context of partition and people she knows and loves pack their belongings and leave. India has been partitioned, and Dighpait has now become a part of a new country — East Pakistan. Forced to leave her beloved house and her friends, especially her brother Majam, Daya resolves never to mention what they have left behind and so from childhood, from adulthood to middle age, she never speaks of Dighpait. Her experience was deep buried in the grave of fine, it was not articulated which is evident in her own words, "The memories of my childhood are completely mine — I vowed never to express them. But at a certain point of time I could bear the burden of them — I had to write" (Sikdar 3).

And then in early 1990s nearly 35 years after experiencing all the memories, when she hears of Majam's death, the floodgates of her memory open. She has created a world of her own – a world utter agony and despair and at the same time with the flicker of little drops of hope oozing sometimes. This zoning of a world of herself completely devoid of the patriarchal demonic face, is similar to the "wild" of the two Oxford cultural anthropologists Shirley and Edwin Ardener who in "Belief and Problem of Women" suggest that:

> Women constitute a 'muted group', the boundaries of whose culture and reality overlap, but are not wholly contained by, the 'dominant (male) group'; there is also a crescent which is outside the dominant boundary and therefore wild. (3)

The book reveals two aspects of her memory — first the sense of trauma for being separated from the village she was brought up by her foster mother in the context of partition, thus she wants to conceal them: and second the sentiment of nostalgia, the element of attachment. Filled with a sense of trauma and tragedy Dayamayee gradually hid her voice and then lost into a paradigm of "silence" surged upon her and this is evident in her labour or projected and manufactured ignorance — to forget her past. She did not want to articulate her memories and to share her heartfelt feelings with this world about which she was sure that nobody would ever understand her. Later her telling of the story she experienced in her girlhood made this novel autobiographical and she substituted her public — identity from Dayamayee to Sunanda.

As a passive and silent observer she witnessed each and every details of Dighpait — commenting on nothing — actually she was 12 then and did not have the reasonable faculty fully grown up — but her innocent questions on the observations sometimes brought the societal framework into serious threat, bringing the marginal into centre. Thus, she talked about the distress of Modi Bhabi, an unfortunate Muslim girl of Dighpait, who loved the Suresh, the son of the village *Morol* (Chief) and she was turned completely unhinged or mad as her lover Suresh is forced to leave her and sent to India/ Hindustan. The desire of a girl did not stop even for the barrier but she sent a *nakshi kāṅthâ* (embroidered blanket) for Suresh. Her memory was inscribed on the blood lingering space and time of partition and the sad story of Modi Bhabi and Suresh recounts that. Then, Dayamayee proceeded to tell the story of another *abhāgi* (unfortunate woman), Bhuli Pishima, her aunt and a widow at ten. When she was a mere child she got married to a sixty year old person who died few days later and the child had to put up with the man made patriarchal barriers — and eventually succumbed to *tirtha darshan* (pilgrimage) by travelling from one place to another.

Much of the charm in Daya's tale lies in the innocent way it was narrated. That young Daya was unable to read books beyond the two epics, she was not allowed to go to school because the boys went there, but Daya learnt some of the poetry and stories by listening to the aloud reading of the boys. She was the reader of Koran for the neighbour Muslim families. And when she was sent in West Bengal to her mother, a school Head mistress forced her to study Engineering without asking what her desire was. Actually every "desire" needs a "voice" — but Daya could not express anything — her words are repressed and suppressed because there was nobody to take her onto the lap and let her express her memories and the shock she got from the separation from her root and this "rootlessness" made her "numb" and "silenced" — either she had to keep in some secret chamber and had to make the emotions and desires expressed through "tears."

Then what is the thread that interweaves Daya and Virmati together? Their story may not run in the same vein and they may not belong to the same cultural territory, even then their agony is weighed in the same parameter — the parameter of "desire to break the barrier." Both they were uprooted from their own selves because of the cancer called partition. Daya could have uttered the words she wanted to but she was silent or in fact she could not because she was on the margin and could not able to transfer herself to the centre as exemplified in the essay "Can the Subaltern Speak?" by Gayatri Chakravorty Spivak that the "subaltern cannot speak. There is no virtue in global laundry list with 'woman' as a pious item. Represention has not withered away. The female intellectual as intellectual has a circumscribed task which she must not disown with a flourish" (308).

But, after a certain period of time nearly thirty-five years after when the small Daya became another woman at the "death" of the "small Daya" (the previous self of Dayamayee) who wanted to suppress her emotions, she let the emotions out of her and gave the small Daya a voice. Similarly Ida the daughter of Virmati came and dug up the lost voice of her mother. What we have is her daughter's reconstruction and representation of her life-story. Thus, at the centre of these narratives we see two women, who fight, but fail, showing that what happens to Virmati and Daya is the general destiny of Indian women.

Works Cited

Ardener, Edwin. "Belief and Problem of Women." *Perceiving Women*. Ed. Shirley Ardener. London: Hammond World Atlas Corp, 1982. Print.

Bhat, Yashoda, and Yamuna Raja Rao, eds. *The Image of Woman in Indian Literature*. New Delhi: B. R. Publishing Corporation, 1993. Print.

Kapur, Manju. *Difficult Daughters*. London: Faber and Faber, 1998. Print.

Malik, Sheema. *Discussing Indian Women Writers: Some Feminist Issues*. New Delhi: R. K. Dhawan and Motini, 2005. Print.

Salvador, Dora Sales. "The Memory of Desire in Manju Kapur's *Difficult Daughters:* In Past and Future Tense." *Memory, Imagination and Desire*. Eds. Constanza del Río and Luis M. García Mainar. Heidelberg: Universitätsverlag Winter, 2004. Print.

Sikdar, Sunanda. *Dayamayeer Katha*. Kolkata: Gangchil, 2008. Print.

Spivak, Gayatri Chakravorty "Can the Subaltern Speak?" *Marxism and the Interpretation of Culture*. Ed. Cary Nelson and Lawrence Grossberg. Chicago U of Illinois P, 1988. 271-313. Print.

IN LIEU OF AN AFTERWORD

It is inordinately difficult to conclude a book with a wide spectrum of literary indulgences joined by the sole thread of female authorship. Therefore, instead of a summation of the preceding chapters, we attempt a furthering of the thematic, with the possibility of future coverage. The individual authors and their selected works presented us with the opportunity to write at length on the possibilities of how their fiction could arguably be used as a possible means of 'reading' the authors themselves or reading into their individualistic modes of fiction the ways that are being employed to dedicate their literary sensibilities into their other related concerns. However, it is also notable that reading individual works as signifiers of the author could prove to be fallacious, and therefore it is also beneficial to keep the authors in perspective, with regard to their body of work, as well as being contextualised at times as 'postcolonial writers', American, Indian, Pakistani, or Bangladeshi authors, postmodern, ecological, activist, acclaimed, third world, urban, diaspora, expatriate, multiethnic, et al— signifiers which could permit genre based divisions to be applicable quite easily and earnestly. But, in order to augment the possibilities of each writer through broader perspectives, we present as an Afterword an accessory which is an intonation of the direction of our future work.

As each chapter has exhaustively covered the dynamics of specific vantage points of each author in terms of standalone works rather than a holistic biographical study or a summative assessment, in this Afterword we present an overview of other important women novelists, albeit an inconveniently limited list, conforming not particularly to the postmodern and postcolonial spheres, and who, regrettably, have been omitted from the present volume. The authors are listed alphabetically, in no specific national or temporal order, and while the limitations of the Afterword curb possibilities of detailed discussions, we shall try to induce introductory statements rather than analytic ones which could be of help to the prospective researcher in a similar area. The list/glossary also includes biographical information in a similar format for authors who have been discussed in this volume as an appendix to their individual works already discussed. Due to the constraints of length, the studies presented here will be very inadequate but we hope to remedy the same in a prospective future volume.

Monica Ali (1967—): Monica Ali is a Bangladesh born British writer and novelist. A former student of philosophy, politics and economics at the Wadham College at the University of Oxford, she was selected as one of the "Best of Young Novelists" by Granta magazine in 2003 based on her then unpublished manuscript of her first novel which was thereafter published as *Brick Lane* (2003). The novel was nominated for the Man Booker Prize and was shortlisted. Since then, Monica Ali has published three more novels: *Alentejo Blue* (2006), *In the Kitchen* (2009), and *Untold Story* (2011).

Margaret Atwood (1939—): Margaret Eleanor Atwood is an acclaimed Canadian novelist, poet, essayist, literary critic, and environmental activist. Her wide range of writing traverses the genres of historical fiction, science fiction, dystopian fiction and speculative fiction. Throughout her career she has shortlisted five times for the Booker Prize, winning it once (2000), as well as the prestigious Arthur c. Clarke Award (1985) and the Prince of Asturias Award for Literature, and was also a founding trustee of the Griffin Poetry Prize. Her notable works of longer fiction include *The Edible Woman* (1969), *Surfacing* (1972), *Lady Oracle* (1976), *The Handmaid's Tale* (1985), *Cat's Eye* (1988), *The Robber Bride* (1993), *Alias Grace* (1996), *The Blind Assassin* (2000), *Oryx and Crake* (2003), *The Penelopiad* (2005), *The Year of the Flood* (2009), and *MaddAddam* (2013).

A.S. Byatt (1936—): Dame Antonia Susan Duffy, known as A.S. Byatt, is a British novelist and poet. Her notable works include *Still Life* (1985, winner of the PEN/Macmillan Silver Pen Award in 1989), the brilliant *Possession* (1990) which won the Man Booker Prize in 1990, and *The Children's Book* (2009),which was shortlisted for the Man Booker Prize and won the James Tait Black Memorial Prize.

Angela Carter (1940-1992): Angela Carter was an English novelist whose works display a blend of feminism, magical realism and picaresque imagery, influenced largely by her own experiences. Her novel *Nights at the Circus* (1984) was the year's winner of the James Tait Black Memorial Prize for fiction and subsequently in 2012 was named the best ever winner of the prize. Her novel *Heroes and Villains* (1969) earned her the Somerset Maugham Award. Her other notable longer works of fiction include: *Shadow Dance* (1966), *The Magic Toyshop* (1967), *Several Perceptions* (1968), *Love* (1971), *The Infernal Desire Machines of Doctor Hoffman* (1972), *The Passion of New Eve* (1977), and *Wise Children* (1991).

Anita Desai (1937—): Anita Desai is an Indian novelist whose works have shown a tendency to proliferate from the localisation of the Indian narratives to a diasporic sensibility that her life abroad has infused in her. She is currently the Emerita John E. Burchard Professor of Humanities at the Massachusetts Institute of Technology. During her prolonged career as a novelist she has been shortlisted thrice for the Booker Prize, received a Sahitya Akademi Award (1978), the Padma Bhushan (2014) and the British Guardian Prize. Her notable works include *Bye-bye Blackbird* (1971), *Clear Light of Day* (1980), *The Village by the Sea* (1982), *Journey to Ithaca* (1995), *Fasting, Feasting* (1999),and *The Zigzag Way* (2004).

Kiran Desai (1971—): Kiran Desai is an Indian author and the daughter of Anita Desai who is known for her novels that explore an Indian psychology that traverses diaspora as well as the effects of the homeland itself. Her most renowned novel is *The Inheritance of Loss* (2006) which won the 2006 Man Booker Prize as well as the 2006 National Book Critics Circle Fiction Award. Her published novel is *Hullabaloo in the Guava Orchard* (1998), which too won notable awards and acclaim, especially from other important authors such as Salman Rushdie.

Shashi Deshpande (1938—): An acclaimed novelist and journalist, Shashi Deshpande is the winner of the Sahitya Akademi Award in 1990 for *That Long Silence*, and the Padma Shri in 2009. Besides her books for children and her numerous short stories and essays Shashi Deshpande has written nine novels so far. Her works include *The Dark Holds No Terror* (1980), *If I Die Today* (1982), *Come Up and Be Dead* (1983), *That Long Silence* (1989), *Moving On* (2004), and *In the Country of Deceit* (2008).

Mahasweta Devi (1926–): Mahasweta (or Mahasveta) Devi is an award winning and acclaimed Indian novelist, short story writer, dramatist, essayist and social activist. Her works of fiction have notably been translated by the postcolonial scholar Gayatri Chakravorty Spivak; these include *Choti Munda and His Arrow* (1980), *Imaginary Maps* (1995), *Bashai Tudu* (1993) and *Breast Stories* (1997). Besides these Spivak has also translated *In Other Worlds: Essays in Cultural Politics* (1987). Mahasweta Devi's works have found a wide audience and readership through these and several other translations as well as the film adaptations that have been made of Devi's works. As an author she has won the Sahitya Akademi Award (1979), the Padma Shri (1986), the Jnanapith Award (1996) and the Ramon Magsaysay Award (1997).

Chitra Bannerjee Divakaruni (1956—): Chitra Bannerjee Divakaruni is an Indian novelist, short story writer, who currently teaches Creative Writing at the University of Houston. She has won numerous awards including the Ginsberg Poetry Prize, the Pushcart Prize, the LA Times Best Books of (1997), the American Book Award, the PEN Oakland/Josephine Miles Literary Award and the South Asian Literary Association Distinguished Author Award. In addition, her novel *Mistress of Spices* won her a nominatioOn for the Orange Prize. Her notable works include *The Mistress of Spices*(1997), *Sister of My Own Heart* (1999), *The Palace of Illsuions* (2008), and *One Amazing Thing* (2010).

Margaret Drabble (1939—): Dame Margaret Drabble, Lady Holroyd is a renowned novelist and critic with eighteen novels published thus far. Her third novel, *The Millstone* (1965), won the John Llewellyn Rhys Memorial Prize in 1966, and *Jerusalem* (1967) won the James Tait Black Memorial Prize in 1967. Her novels are infused with realism, the tragic intensity of the characters falling apart due to individual and political issues at hand. Her writing also speaks of her knowledge of novelists that she has widely critiqued, including Thomas Hardy and Iris Murdoch.

Manju Kapur (1948—): An Indian novelist, Manju Kapur is the winner of the Commonwealth Writers' Prize for best first book in 1999 for her novel, *Difficult Daughters* (1998). Her later novels include *A Married Woman* (2003), *Home* (2006), *The Immigrant* (2008), and *Custody* (2011). Her novel, *The Immigrant* was shortlisted for the DSC Prize for South Asian Literature in 2011.

Jhumpa Lahiri (1967—): Jhumpa Lahiri is an Indian American author. Her first published work, *Interpreter of Maladies* (1999), a collection of short stories, won the 2000 Pulitzer Prize for Fiction. She has since published another collection of short stories, *Unaccustomed Earth* (2008), and two novels, *The Namesake* (2003) and *The Lowland* (2014), with the latter being a nominee for the Man Booker Prize and the National Book Award for Fiction. She is also the recipient of the PEN/Hemingway Award for fiction in 1999, a Guggenheim Fellowship in 2002, an Asian American Literary Award in 2009 and the Premio Gregor von Rezzori for translated fiction in 2009.

Doris Lessing (1919-2013): Doris Lessing was an extremely variegated, almost multidisciplinary, literary practitioner whose creative genres included novels, poems, plays, librettos, biographies and short stories. Two of her most notable novels are *The Grass is Singing* (1950) and *The Golden Notebook* (1962), which only form an iota of her vast output. She has been the recipient of the Nobel Prize in Literature in 2007 besides the Somerset Maugham Award in 1954 and the James Tait Black Memorial Prize in 1995.

Toni Morrison (1931—): Toni Morrison is an American novelist, professor and Nobel laureate, whose works have been noted for their "epic themes, vivid dialogue and richly detailed characters". She has been a winner of the Pulitzer Prize for Fiction and the American Book Award in 1988 for *Beloved* (1987), and the Nobel Prize for Literature in 1993. Her other notable works f fiction include *The Bluest Eye* (1970), *Sula* (1973), *Song of Solomon* (1977), *Tar Baby* (1981), *Jazz* (1992), *Paradise* (1997), *Love* (2003), *A Mercy* (2008) and *Home* (2012). She has been a recipient of the National Book Critics Circle Award in 1977 and the National Humanities Medal in 2000.

Bharati Mukherjee (1940—): Bharati Mukherjee is an Indian American author and professor of English at the University of California, Berkeley. She does not consider herself as part of the Indian diasporic literary phenomenon but as a wholly American author writing on Indian or Indian-American issues. Thus far she has written eight novels, they are: *The Tiger's Daughter* (1971), *Wife* (1975), *Jasmine* (1989), *The Holder of the World* (1993), *Leave it to Me* (1997), *Desirable Daughters* (2002), *The Tree Bride* (2004), and *Miss New India* (2011). She has been a recipient of the National Book Critics Circle Award in 1988.

Iris Murdoch (1919-99): Iris Murdoch was a British-Irish author and philosopher whose novels dealt with issues such as sexuality and sexual relationships, morality, good and evil and psychological issues. She is consistently ranked among the best British novelists of her age. Some of her notable works include *Under the Net* (1954), *The Bell* (1958), *The Severed Head* (1961), *The Black Prince* (1973, winner of the James Tait Black Memorial Prize), *The Sacred and Profane Love* (1974, winner of the Whitbread literary award for fiction), *The Sea, the Sea* (1978, winner of the Booker Prize), and *The Good Apprentice* (1985) among others.

Taslima Nasrin (1963—): Taslima Nasrin is a Bangladeshi author who is renowned for her fiction that revolves around feminist issues and criticism and religious ideologies that encumber the society by asserting dogma and patriarchy. She currently resides in New Delhi, India, following several threats made on her after the publication of her novels and memoirs. Although Nasrin writes in Bengali, her works have been widely translated into several other languages including English. Nasrin's most acclaimed and controversial work is *Lajja* (or *Shame*) published in 1993. The novel dealt with the persecution of a Hindu family by Muslims. Following the publication of the novel Nasrin was subjected to attacks and threats which resulted in her escape to Sweden by the end of 1994. Her novels have been translated into English as: *The Opponent* (1992), *Invitation* (1993), *Return* (1993), *Tell Him the Secret* (1994), *French Lover* (2002), and *Shame Again* (2009). She has a recipient of the Simone de Beauvoir Prize for her contribution to the advancement of feminist causes.

Jean Rhys (1890-1979): Jean Rhys was a mid-twentieth century novelist, short story writer and essayist whose seminal work, *Wide Sargasso Sea* (1966) was written as a "prequel" to Charlotte Brontë's *Jane Eyre*. Her Welsh-Creole origins and her upbringing in Dominica made her more of a postcolonial litterateur than other women authors who had similarly been writing while based in England in her contemporary period. Her other notable works include *Good Morning, Midnight* (1939), *Sleep It Off Lady* (1976) among others.

J.K. Rowling (1965—): Joanne Rowling, also known by her pen names J.K. Rowling and Robert Galbraith, is a British novelist most well known for her series of Harry Potter novels, arguably some of the century's best selling and most popular books. Rowling has written altogether seven books in the Harry Potter series: *Harry Potter and the Philosopher's Stone* (1997), *Harry Potter and the Chamber of Secrets* (1998), *Harry Potter and the Prisoner of Azkaban* (1999), *Harry Potter and the Goblet of Fire* (2000), *Harry Potter and the Order of the Phoenix* (2003), *Harry Potter and the Half-Blood Prince* (2005), and *Harry Potter and the Deathly Hallows* (2007). The books have been adapted into a successful cinematic franchise and other commercial products, besides Rowling's penning additional books to compliment or supplement the original series. Rowling has since then turns towards writing books for adults, with her first book being *The Casual Vacancy* (2012), and subsequently two further books as Robert Galbraith: *The Cuckoo's Calling* (2013) and *The Silkworm* (2014)— both of which belong to the Cormoran Strike series.

Arundhati Roy (1961—): Arundhati Roy is an Indian author and political activist who is best known for her novel *The God of Small Things* which won the 1998 Man Booker Prize for Fiction. She is also an environmental and human rights activist. Before turning to her foray into writing fiction, of which only her single acclaimed novel exists, Roy wrote screenplays for numerous films as well. *The God of Small Things* was a semi-autobiographical work which dealt with her life and childhood experiences in Aymanam. Since the publication of her debut novel in 1997, Roy has stated that she is working on a new novel and has written several books of essays, cultural criticism and writings charged with activism to the tune of her personal activities.

Nayantara Sahgal (1927—): Nayantara Sahgal is an Indian author of fiction in English who focuses on the rise of India's opulence, or its localisation in certain elite classes, and the changes wrought by such a meteoric rise of the elite class. Her novels are political commentaries, social commentaries and also motivated in terms of exploring gender issues. She was awarded the Sahitya Akademi Award for English in 1986 for her novel, *Rich Like Us* (1985). Her other notable works include a memoir, *Prison and Chocolate* (1954), *From Fear Set Free* (1963), *A Time to Be Happy* (1963), *This Time of Morning* (1965), *Storm in Chandigarh* (1969), *Sunlight Surrounds You* (1970;with Chandralekha Mehta and Rita Dar), *The Day in Shadow* (1971), *Indira Gandhi: Her Road to Power* (1982), *Plans for Departure* (1985), *Mistaken Identity* (1988), *A Situation in New Delhi* (1989), and *Lesser Breeds* (2003).

Bapsi Sidhwa (1938—): Bapsi Sidhwa is an American author of Pakistani origin who is widely known for her collaborations with the Indo-Canadian filmmaker Deepa Mehta. Sidhwa's works of fiction show an inclination to document the experience of partition and her reminiscences of the movement for freedom. Her works of fiction include *The Crow Eaters* (1979), *The Bride* (1982), *Cracking India* (1991; also known as *Ice Candy Man*), *An American Brat* (1993), *Water: A Novel* (2006), and *Their Language of Love* (2013). Besides her prolific writing career, Sidhwa has taught at the University of Houston, Rice University, Columbia University, Mount Holyoke College, and Brandeis University.

Zadie Smith (1975—): Zadie Smith is an English novelist, essayist and short story writer with four hugely acclaimed novels thus far. She has won the Orange Prize for Fiction in 2006. Her novels are *White Teeth* (2000), which thrust her into the literary world as a definite tour de force, *The Autograph Man* (2002), *On Beauty* (2005) and *NW* (2012) besides the novella, *The Embassy of Cambodia* (2013). Her novels infuse elements of Postcoloniality, postmodernity and other contemporary cultural amplifications that serve towards bringing into the fore the experience of the population that she tries to bring through.

Alice Walker (1944—): Alice Walker is an American author who is best known for her novel *The Color Purple* (1982). Her novels and other writings have dealt with issues pertaining largely to the status of the 'black' woman. Exploitation of the woman doubly— once as a woman and then as back is one of the core issues of her novels, especially *The Color Purple*. Some of her other works include *The Third Life of Grange Copeland* (1970), *Meridian* (1976), and *Possessing the Secret of Joy* (1992) among others. For *The Color Purple*, Walker has won the Pulitzer Prize for Fiction (1983) and the National Book Award for fiction (1983).

BIBLIOGRAPHY

This is a general reading list. The works cited sections for each chapter, including the Introduction, provides a detailed list of sources and resources utilised in the compilation of the present volume, whereas this bibliography is provided for readers who may be interested in further reading on women's issues and women's writing. The list contains both familiar and less known names of authors and books, but a very essential corpus of women's issues and writing. This is not a holistic list and should not be treated as one either. However, concerns of postcolonial feminism, South Asian women's studies and other relatively later developments in women's studies are well covered in the following volumes which will act as complete resources for scholars attempting to research on the works of women authors, poets, playwrights, women's issues and studies of women both in the third world and in the post-global world.

Bagchi, Jashodhara (ed.). *India Women: Myth and Reality*. Hyderabad: Sangam Books, 1995. Print.

Barrett, Michèle (ed.). *Women and Writing*. London: Women's Press, 1979. Print.

Battersby, Christina. *Gender and Genius: Toward a Feminist Aesthetics*. London: Women's Press, 1989. Print.

Beauvoir, Simone de. *The Second Sex*, trans. H.M. Parshley. New York: Knopf, 1953. Print.

Bhattacharjee, Subashish, Saikat Guha and Mandika Sinha (eds.). *Reading Literature through Feminist Lens: Theory and Praxis*. New Delhi: Authorspress, 2015. Print.

Bowden, Peta and Jane Mummery. *Understanding Feminism*. Durham: Acumen, 2009.Print.

Bowlby, Rachel (ed.). *A Woman's Essays*. Harmondsworth: Penguin, 1992. Print.

Butler, Judith. *Gender Trouble: Feminism and the Subversion of Identity*. New York: Routledge, 1991. Print.

Chakraverty, Lalima. *Gender and Culture in the Works of Indian Continent's Select Women Novelists*. New Delhi: Atlantic, 2012. Print.

Chaudhuri, Maitrayee (ed.). *Feminism in India*. New Delhi: Kali for Women, 2004. Print.

Cornillon, Susan Koppelman (ed.). *Images of Women in Fiction*. Bowling Green, Ohio: University Popular Press, 1972. Print.

Fetterley, Judith. *The Resisting Reader: A Feminist Approach to American Fiction*. Bloomington: Indiana University Press, 1978. Print.

Forbes, Geraldine. *Women in Modern India*. Cambridge: Cambridge University Press, 1999. Print.

Genz, Stéphanie and Benjamin A. Brabon. *Postfeminism: Cultural Texts and Theories*. Edinburgh: Edinburgh University Press, 2009. Print.

Ghadially, Rehana. *Women in Indian Society*. New Delhi: Sage Publications, 1988. Print.

Gilbert, Sandra and Susan Gubar. *No Man's Land: The Place of the Women Writer in the Twentieth Century, Vol. I: The War of the Words*. New Haven: Yale University Press, 1988. Print.

—. *No Man's Land: The Place of the Women Writer in the Twentieth Century, Vol. II: Sexchanges*. New Haven: Yale University Press, 1989. Print.

—. *No Man's Land: The Place of the Women Writer in the Twentieth Century, Vol. III: Letters From the Front*. New Haven: Yale University Press, 1994. Print.

— (ed.). *The Norton Anthology of Literature by Women*. New York: Norton, 1996. Print.

Glover, David and Cora Kaplan. *Genders*, 2nd Edition. Oxon and New York: Routledge, 2009. Print. The New Critical Idiom.

Gubar, Susan. *Critical Condition: Feminism at the Turn of the Century*. New York and West Sussex: Columbia University Press, 2000. Print.

Jackson, Stevi and Jackie Jones (ed.). *Contemporary Feminist Theories*. Edinburgh: Edinburgh University Press, 1998. Print.

John, Mary E. (ed.). *Women's Studies in India: A Reader*. New Delhi: Penguin, 2008. Print.

Kaplan, Cora. *The Erotics of Talk: Women's Writing and Feminist Paradigms*. New York: Oxford University press, 1996. Print.

Kauffman, Linda (ed.). *Gender and Theory: Dialogues on Feminist Criticism*. Oxford: Basil Blackwell, 1989. Print.

Kiberd, Declan. *Men and Feminism in Modern Literature*. Delhi: Macmillan Press, 1985. Print.

Kime Scott, Bonnie (ed.). *The Gender of Modernism*. Bloomington: Indiana University Press, 1990. Print.

—. *Refiguring Modernism 1: The Women of 1928*. Bloomington: Indiana University Press, 1995a. Print.

—. *Refiguring Modernism 2: Postmodern Feminist readings of Woolf, West and Barnes*. Bloomington: Indiana University Press, 1995b. Print.

Kumar, Radha. *The History of Doing: An Illustrated Account of Movements for Women's Rights and Feminism in India, 1800-1990*. New Delhi: Zubaan, 2011. Print.

McCann, Carole R. and Seung-kyung Kim. *Feminist Theory Reader: Local and Global Perspectives*. New York and Oxon: Routledge, 2010. Print.

Menon, Nivedita. *Recovering Subversion: Feminist Politics Beyond the Law*. New Delhi: Permanent Black, 2007. Print.

—. *Seeing Like a Feminist*. New Delhi: Penguin, 2012. Print.

Minh-ha, Trinh T. *Women, Native, Other*. Bloomington: Indiana University Press, 1989. Print.

Mohanty, Chandra Talpade. *Feminism Without Borders*. New Delhi: Zubaan, 2003. Print.

Moi, Toril. *Sexual/Textual Politics: Feminist Literary Theory*. London: Methuen, 1985. Print.

Ray, Girindra Narayan and Jaydip Sarkar (eds.). *The Postcolonial Woman Question: Readings in Indian Women Novelists in English*. Kolkata: Books Way, 2011. Print.

Riley, Denise. *"Am I That Name?": Feminism and the Category of 'Women' in History*. Minneapolis: University of Minnesota Press, 1988. Print.

Rooney, Ellen (ed.). *The Cambridge Companion to Feminist Literary Theory*. Cambridge: Cambridge University Press, 2006. Print.

Ruthven, K.K. *Feminist Literary Studies: An Introduction*. Cambridge: Cambridge University Press, 1984. Print.

Sangari, K and S. Vaid. *Recasting Women*. New Delhi: Kali for Women, 1989. Print.

Showalter, Elaine (ed.). *The New Feminist Criticism: Essays on Women, Literature, and Theory*. New York: Pantheon, 1985. Print.

—. *A Literature of Their Own: English Women Novelists from Brontë to Lessing*. London: Virago, 2003 [1977]. Print.

Singh, Charu Sheel. *Women about Women in Indian Literature in English*. New Delhi: Anmol Publications, 1998. Print.

Singh, Jyoti. *Indian Women Novelists*. New Delhi: Rawat Publications, 2007. Print.

Singh, Nisha Chandra. *Radical Feminism and Women's Writing*. New Delhi: Atlantic, 2007. Print.

Spencer, Jane. *The Rise of the Woman Novelist: From Aphra Behn to Jane Austen*. Oxford: Blackwell, 1986. Print.

Spivak, Gayatri Chakravorty. *In Other Worlds: Essays in Cultural Politics*. New York: Routledge, 1988. Print.

—. *Outside in the Teaching Machine*. New York: Routledge, 1993. Print.

Stubbs, Patricia. *Women and Fiction, 1880-1920*. Brighton: Harvester, 1979. Print.

Swain, S.P. *The Feminine Voice in Indian Fiction*. New Delhi: Asia Book Club, 2000. Print.

Tharu, Susie and K. Lalitha (eds.). *Women Writing in India, Vol. I*. New Delhi: Oxford University Press, 1991. Print.

Walters, Margaret. *Feminism: A Very Short Introduction*. Oxford: Oxford University Press, 2006. Print.

Woodward, Kath. *The Short Guide to Gender*. Bristol: The Policy Press, 2010. Print.

Woolf, Virginia. *A Room of One's Own*. Oxford: Oxford University Press, 1998 [1929]. Print.